D1398610

Weekend Wisdom
2000

Weekend Wisdom 2000

Home advice, tips and timesavers
to make your life easier
from
The Daily Telegraph readers

Introduction by
Susannah Charlton

Robinson
IN COLLABORATION WITH
THE DAILY TELEGRAPH

Robinson Publishing Ltd
7 Kensington Church Court
London W8 4SP

First published by Robinson Publishing Ltd 1999
Selection and editorial material © *The Daily Telegraph* 1998,1999
Textual copyright © Various. All rights reserved.

A copy of the British Library Cataloguing in Publication Data
for this title is available from the British Library

ISBN 1-84119-114-0

Edited and designed by
OutHouse Publishing Services
Line-drawings by Gillian Martin

Printed and bound in Finland by WSOY

Disclaimer
The following tips have been sent in by readers of
The Daily Telegraph's Weekend section and are not endorsed
in any way by either the Publishers or *The Daily Telegraph*.

Contents

Introduction

As Wisdoms continue to flood into the Weekend office week by week, it has become clearer than ever that *The Daily Telegraph* readers are an inexhaustible source of practical, inventive ideas and applied common sense. After the enthusiastic reception given to the first *Weekend Wisdom* anthology, we are delighted to present this new collection of tips and advice to help make life easier in the new millennium.

We may be about to enter the twenty-first century, but the old-fashioned everyday problems haven't gone away: how *do* you get rid of scorch marks, keep slugs out of your pot plants, dry woollies without pulling them out of shape, or get old putty out of a window-frame? Then there are those more unusual dilemmas – not all of us will have wrestled with the difficulty of grooming a hamster, staying warm on a cold cricket pitch, amusing a bored horse or recycling used engine oil.

As well as the practical tips, we have included some from the boundaries of common sense. Who are we to say that they don't contain a kernel of wisdom? And they will certainly make you smile, even though you may not leap at the idea of putting up plastic owls to keep pigeons and seagulls away from your house, or watching television through binoculars!

One of the really cheering things about this book is the sense of people striking back at the nuisances of modern life – fobbing off muggers with out-of-date credit-cards, sniffing out dodgy car dealers over the phone, dealing with dusty televisions and fading batteries – with a real determination that's not to be outdone.

From traditional wisdom that has been handed down from mother to daughter, and father to son, to ingenious recycling ideas for coping with the detritus of modern living, *The Daily Telegraph* readers have generously shared their store of knowledge with us all. We are immensely grateful to all those readers who have allowed their useful and illuminating Wisdoms to be included in this anthology.

Susannah Charlton
Telegraph Books

Around the House

Clean an eggy or milky pastry brush by placing it in cold water as soon as possible after use, and before washing. (Since egg contains protein, it sets in hot water.)

Sheila Green, Honiton, Devon

Use your baby-bottle steam steriliser to sterilise your jars for jam-making. Quick and simple.

Mrs V Barratt, Doncaster, South Yorkshire

Keep a firm toothbrush in your sink-tidy, and use it to clean graters and herb-mills quickly and efficiently.

G Morgan, Berkeley, Gloucestershire

A quick way to clean a cheese-grater is to grate a piece of stale bread immediately after grating the cheese.

Pat McNeil, Coleshill, Buckinghamshire

To remove stains from plastic kettles, fill the kettle with water, add three slices of lemon, boil, and leave overnight. Rinse the next morning.

S N MacArthur, London

Remove stains from any teapot by filling it with boiling water and two tablespoons of washing soda. Leave for an hour or two, and then rinse away all the stains with a brush.

Irene Pitt, Glasgow

To remove tea-stains from china cups and saucers, rub common salt onto them with a damp cloth, and rinse.

Mrs L Hargrave, North Petherton, Somerset

ᔥ

Furniture polish will penetrate wood more easily if the container is first warmed in a bowl of hot water.

Neil Wraigh, Millom, Cumbria

For a clean, clear shine on your furniture, polish with vinegar.

Mrs Jane Cook, Exeter, Devon

Use salt water to clean wicker furniture or clothes-baskets. Allow them to dry naturally outdoors in the sun.

K Green, London

Coat the underside of a new wooden lavatory-seat with a clear varnish. This will make it easier to keep clean.

Sheila Smith, Coulsdon, Surrey

ᔥ

To remove heat-marks from a polished table, rub with mayonnaise and polish with a soft cloth.

M L Lucas, Bushmills, Co Antrim

To make scratch-marks on furniture permanently invisible, rub baby oil or cooking oil over them every hour or two for a few hours.

Mrs J Connell, Walton-on-Thames, Surrey

Scratches on wooden furniture will vanish when rubbed with half a brazil nut.

Cindy Wolfenden, Southampton, Hampshire

Correction fluid is very handy for touching up scratches and knocks on white kitchen appliances and paintwork.

Jean Lepla, Gerrards Cross, Buckinghamshire

Repair a small nick in glassware by rubbing it with an emery-board nail-file. It will smooth out jagged edges in minutes.

Sheila Smith, Coulsdon, Surrey

ॐ

Does your milk-jug drip and leave milky ring-marks? Put a very small amount of butter around the edge of the lip.

Mrs J Moss, Portishead, North Somerset

To prevent bottles of sauce becoming sticky, rinse the cap before replacing it.

Miss L C Hinton, Taunton, Devon

ॐ

To speed the polishing of any silver or silver-plated objects, first fill them with very hot water.

Mrs E L Orwin, Bedford

To avoid leaving finger-marks that are then hard to remove, wear plastic, not rubber, gloves when polishing silver .

Mrs L Kettle, St Albans, Hertfordshire

To clean small silver items, place them in a pan of boiling water with some aluminium foil. Drain, and then allow to dry thoroughly.

Christine Carpenter, London

To clean up tarnished copper or brass, smother the item with Worcestershire sauce and then rub it vigorously. When the marks have disappeared, you can restore the shine with brass polish.

J Doxat, Camberley, Surrey

Clean chrome with baby oil, club soda, or lemon juice, and then polish to a shine with a soft cloth.

Mrs L Kettle, St Albans, Hertfordshire

Clean chrome – or any white metal – with toothpaste.

Sarah Parkinson, Stroud, Gloucestershire

Clean pewter by rubbing it with cabbage leaves.

Mrs Gwen Howell, London

Do not store pewter in oak cupboards: oak gives off fumes that corrode the metal.

Mrs A Goodacre, Lincoln

Don't allow pampas grass near silver – the pollen makes ineradicable, black tarnish-marks.

C McKillop, Kingsbridge, Devon

ଚ୨

To clean the glass roof of your conservatory, squirt washing-up liquid onto it from an upstairs window just before heavy rain.

R F Smith, Hatfield, Hertfordshire

Add a squirt of washing-up liquid, and one squirt of vinegar, to a plastic spray-bottle full of water – excellent for cleaning windows.

Mr & Mrs I L Williams, Saundersfoot, Dyfed

ဆာ

To keep your chimney clear of soot, burn a mixture of salt and potato-peelings in the grate once a week.

George Hopwood, Whitefield, Manchester

Revive a flat broom by placing it in a bucket of salt water and leaving it until it is thoroughly soaked: the bristles will stand up stiff and straight again.

Brian Gilbert, Kingswells, Aberdeen

You can prevent your paths from becoming slippery by brushing them with a very weak solution of Jeyes fluid.

Mrs M Snapes, Sevenoaks, Kent

Cheap pickling vinegar clears cement-stains from brickwork, and also cleans block-paving stones.

D Calderbank, Bolton, Lancashire

Snow will slide off a shovel that is first sprayed with furniture polish or vegetable oil.

J Norris, Corsham, Wiltshire

ဆာ

To prevent food from spitting onto your cooker top, cover the unused area of the hob with tin-foil.

Mrs D Alexander, Peterborough, Cambridgeshire

To clean the interior of a microwave oven, place a bowl of water inside on full power for five minutes. The steam will soften the stains, which can then be wiped away with a clean damp cloth.

Mrs B Hargreaves, Rugby, Warwickshire

Burnt-on splashes on the glass door of your oven? Rubbing with a ball of scrunched-up foil will remove even long-standing marks.

Mrs M Huntington, Workington, Cumbria

After cleaning your oven's enamel interior, apply baking soda with a damp cloth: the grease will lift off easily next time you clean it.

Enid Shaw, Builth Wells, Powys

৪১

To keep the tops of your kitchen cupboards clean, line them with newspaper. When they become greasy or dirty, simply replace the paper.

Karen Fletcher, Croydon

To clean a white fibreglass sink, fill it with hot water and washing powder, and leave it overnight. The result is better than that achieved with bleach!

Mrs V Janin, Bournemouth, Dorset

৪১

To stop a wire-scourer from rusting – and thus prolong its life – wrap it in foil.

Mrs S Morton, Lincoln

If you run out of dishwasher salt, ordinary cooking salt can be used in an emergency.

Mrs Gillian Pearce, Kingston Seymour, Somerset

Rather than buying expensive kitchen disinfectant and cleaner, keep a well-diluted solution of household bleach in a spray container and use that instead.

Helen Love, Lisburn

When moving house, tape spare bags to the vacuum cleaner to avoid an endless search when the inevitable cleaning begins.

Brian Richards, Northiam, East Sussex

ဆ

To clear up smashed raw egg, cover with salt, and leave until the liquid is absorbed; it will then sweep up easily.

Mrs J Dalamine, Bromley, Kent

Pick up broken glass safely and effectively with wet cotton wool.

Emily L Mallard, Cirencester, Gloucestershire

Use a thick slice of bread to pick up broken glass or crockery.

J Cater, Nottingham

To remove the smallest shards of broken glass from the carpet, press a strip of sticky tape onto them.

A Smith, Tarporley, Cheshire

Soot from an open coal fire can be removed from the carpet or hearth-rug by pressing a piece of sticky tape onto it.

Mrs K Conn, Colchester, Essex

❧

To ensure that wooden drawers don't stick, rub them with soap from time to time.

Mrs Helen Wren, Boston, Lancashire

To make wooden drawers open and close more smoothly, rub the runners with a candle.

Angela Bennett, London

If the wind rattles a letterbox or air-vent, muffle the irritating noise by sticking draught-excluding strips along the edges.

M Royle, Selby, North Yorks

A couple of knots in the clothes-line, a few inches apart, will prevent the prop from slipping on windy days.

Mrs Y Martin, Lytham St Annes, Lancashire

❧

Clingfilm is very much easier to use if it is kept in the fridge.

Mrs A G Roberts, Darlington, Co Durham

Make the edge of the clingfilm roll easier to find by making a small fold in it, as you would with sticky tape.

D Fulford, London

To remove the sticky residue left by labels, price-stickers, and old adhesive tape, wipe with a tissue or piece of cloth soaked in lighter fuel. (It works on most surfaces – even paper.)

John H Shaw, London

To remove the glue left on glass by price-stickers, spray with furniture polish and rub gently with a dry cloth.

Mrs B Purvis, Whitby, North Yorkshire

For easy removal of non-water-soluble labels, fill the container with hot water, leave to stand for a couple of minutes, and then simply peel off.

C M Kraemer, Abingdon, Oxon

∞

To force a plastic or metal pipe onto a tube, such as a hose-reel, first plunge the pipe into boiling water for approximately half a minute.

J Rothwell, Lytham St Annes, Lancashire

To make a cork fit easily into a bottle, place the cork in boiling water for a few minutes until it softens.

Mrs S Jones, Princes Risborough, Buckinghamshire

If a candle is too large for a particular candlestick, use a potato-peeler to shave off layers of wax until it fits.

Carolyn Hallinger, Andover, Hampshire

If a roller towel is jammed, pull the rear section of the towel down, rather than the front, until you hear the click as it releases.

C J Taylor, Bristol, Somerset

To remove a tight metal jam-pot lid, invert it in a pan of hot water for half a minute. Place a cloth over it, and simply twist it off.

Eileen Nunn, Weston-Super-Mare, Somerset

To unscrew the tight lid of a glass jar, roll the jar carefully under the ball of your foot. This will release the vacuum.

Mrs F M Fletcher, Hornsea, East Yorkshire

℘

Remove blue/green stains made by dripping taps on a bath by rubbing them with a piece of lemon.

F Tindale, Fulford, Yorkshire

If water is slow to run out of the kitchen sink, cup the palms of your hands over the plug-hole and use as a plunger.

Mrs M Haworth, Sherborne, Dorset

To avoid steaming up the bathroom, run a small quantity of cold water into the bath before turning on the hot tap.

John Mulliner, Southport, Merseyside

Put a clean seashell inside a non-electric kettle to stop it from furring up.

Mrs J A Bristow, Littlehampton, East Sussex

In hard-water areas, collect and filter rainwater for use in your steam iron. This will prevent the iron from 'chalking up'.

R D Nelson, Basingstoke, Hampshire

To save water, collect the cold-water run-off before the hot water comes through. Reserve the cold for future use.

Mrs Barbara Lebbon, Bridgwater, Somerset

You can increase the efficiency of your radiators by placing tin-foil on the wall behind them to re-flect the heat back into the room.

Mrs Alma Shell, Alnwick, Northumberland

∞

An old shaving brush makes a super duster for your china ornaments.

A Henderson, Comrie, Perthshire

Cut the top off a large plastic bottle about three quarters of the way up, invert it, and you have an excellent kitchen funnel.

Richard Wyndham, Marlingford, Norwich

Utilise surplus coat-hangers by removing and reshaping the hook part into an 'S' shape for use as a hook around the house and garden.

V I Bettany, Newark, Nottinghamshire

Pieces of dried orange-peel make excellent fire-lighters.

Mary Falconer, Stroud, Gloucestershire

৪১

Keep a ceramic tile and an impermanent pen by the telephone and use it for writing down messages – it will wipe clean afterwards.

Charlotte Primrose, Newcastle, Staffordshire

To avoid the frustration of searching for the end of a roll of sticky tape, attach a paper-clip to it.

M S, Reading, Berkshire

Use toothpaste to hang posters: it washes off with a damp cloth and won't leave stains.

Mrs Y Martin, Lytham St Annes, Lancashire

Before throwing old rubber gloves away, cut the cuffs off to make large, strong rubber bands.

Mrs John Allen, Henley-on-Thames, Oxon

Slice up a discarded bicycle inner-tube to make countless rubber bands.

Gladys Carter, Stokenchurch, Buckinghamshire

Use the white gummed edges of postage-stamp strips as labels – ideal for home freezing or labelling homemade jam.

Mrs A Burrell, Rochester, Kent

Don't lick the unpleasant, gluey back of stamps; lick the corner of the envelope instead.

Lyn Orton, Epping, Essex

An envelope sealed with the white of an egg cannot be steamed open.

Mrs Carolyn Moore, Westward Ho, North Devon

Old cocoa-tins make light, strong containers for sending small items in the post.

Warren Little, Enniskillen, Northern Ireland

Before punching holes in a document to be filed in a ring-binder, apply adhesive tape to one edge to prevent the paper from tearing.

Mrs E M Caldecott, Norwich, Norfolk

To restart a stalled ballpoint pen, immerse the point in hot water for about fifteen seconds.

Patrick Sullivan, Richmond, Surrey

ℰℴ

If a battery is too small for a machine, you can temporarily bridge the gap between battery and contact points with scrunched-up foil.

L Moxen, Barnstaple, Devon

If a battery no longer has the power necessary to run a radio or shaver, transfer it to an alarm clock and it will last for months.

K D Barritt, Ashstead, Surrey

If you send your camera film to the developers by post, take a photograph of your own name and address on one frame: in the event of loss, the prints can be identified and returned.

Mrs Amina Hannam, Stow-on-the-Wold,
Gloucestershire

An ink-jet cartridge that appears to be empty can usually be revived by removing it from the machine and, holding it horizontally, carefully shaking it from side to side before putting it back.

M J Tunnicliffe, Birmingham, West Midlands

Spray faded typewriter-ribbon with WD40 to renew the oil used in the typewriter ink, and so prolong the ribbon's life.

A A Berry, Grimsby, Lincolnshire

Your PC mouse will run more smoothly if you rub the ball underneath and the mouse mat with a sheet of fabric-conditioner.

Ms Jennifer Smith, Coulsdon, Surrey

ം

To keep your television screen dust- and static-free, wipe it with an anti-static sheet of fabric-softener.

Sheila Smith, Coulsdon, Surrey

For cinema-quality sound from a small television, listen on headphones.

Mrs Jean Davidson, Southend on Sea, Essex

For quick reference, write the names and numbers
of your favourite satellite channels on an adhesive
label stuck to the back of your remote control.

Mrs B Jones, Exeter, Devon

Spiders, and unwelcome insects such as flies, will
cling to the fibres of a fluffy duster, which is then
easily shaken out of the window.

J Royle, Selby, Yorkshire

To keep your house free from mites, spray daily
with essential oils of lavender and geranium. (Add
twenty drops of each to a pint of water.)

Rosemary Eustace, Malvern, Worcestershire

23

To rid your house of ants, first vacuum them up, and then put talcum powder down the cracks as a deterrent. It's as effective as ant powder.

Mrs D Major, Shrewsbury, Shropshire

You can discourage ants by leaving a few cloves on the kitchen surfaces.

Susan Webster, Derby

To keep flies out of the house in summer, light up a fragrant joss-stick or two.

D K Bonnett, Exeter, Devon

Do not clean outside windowsills with a lemon-scented cleaner as it attracts flies.

Mrs J A Green, Chester, Cheshire

Basil grown in a pot on the kitchen windowsill helps to keep flies away.

Mrs Joan Mead, Northampton

To destroy wasps' nests in old brick walls, douse them with hairspray.

H Bishop, Leominster, Hertfordshire

Place mothballs on top of your infra-red burglar-alarm sensors to deter insects from coming too close and setting them off.

Julia Peduzzi, Beckenham, Kent

Brush cobwebs upwards to prevent them from leaving black marks on the wall.

C M Page-Turner, Honiton, Devon

To stop mice getting back into the house through their old holes, block them up with metal scouring pads (they're unchewable).

J Carriss, Bradford, West Yorkshire

Two to three drops of olbas or eucalyptus oil on a tissue inserted in a refuse sack will discourage foxes and cats from ripping into them.

Mrs J Peek, Southsea, Hampshire

To prevent birds from flying into windows or glass doors, tie fluttering ribbons to canes or bushes immediately outside.

Mrs J Burley, Colyton, East Devon

෨

If you can't find freezer-bag ties, cut a strip off the top of the bag and use this instead.

Valerie Jenkins, Black Notley, Essex

When defrosting an upright freezer, drape a towel from the bottom shelf into a bowl. The water will then drain into the bowl, and not onto the floor.

Cedric Harris, Tiverton, Devon

To speed the defrosting of a badly iced-up freezer, place a bowl of very hot (just-boiled) water on the shelf or in one of the basket containers. Then close the door and leave for five minutes.

Mrs N Brookes, Macclesfield, Cheshire

To protect your hands from freezer-burn, wear rubber gloves when emptying the freezer ready for defrosting.

Mrs S Bunn, Tonbridge, Kent

25

When defrosting the fridge or freezer, transfer the food to large thermos-style cooler bags containing two frozen ice-packs. It will stay freezer-cold for two hours.

Mrs Pamela Luck, London

When disposing of an old freezer, keep the plastic drawers and use them to store cleaning materials under the sink.

Christopher & Elaine Ashby, Newark, Nottinghamshire

ജ

Stop your cushions from sliding off the sofa by placing a length of carpet, pile-side up, underneath them.

J A Briggs, Worthing, West Sussex

Stitch a small cross in the centre of the top edge of sheets and blankets for easy positioning when making beds.

Mrs J Warner, Bognor Regis, West Sussex

Large items of household linen are much easier to fold neatly if you stand facing a full-length mirror.

Mrs Agnes Barr, Maidstone, Kent

To improve the whiteness of cotton sheets, hang them out to dry in frosty weather.

Mrs M Pickles, Clitheroe, Lancashire

If washing-line space is limited, peg towels and tea-towels to the bottom edge of those already on the line.

Mrs P Barnham, Cuffley, Hertfordshire

Put your tennis balls in the tumble-dryer when drying pillows, duvets or padded clothes – they will dry as fluffy as new.

Mrs P Hope, Stockbridge, Hampshire

৳৩

Keep two needles threaded, one white, one black, ready for last-minute emergencies.

Mrs E A Churn, Halifax, Yorkshire

It is easier to thread a fine needle if you cut the thread on the cross.

Mrs Margaret Standerline, Matlock, Derbyshire

To thread a needle, lick the eye of the needle, not the cotton.

Jane Stones, Cobham, Surrey

Threading a needle is made easier if you first coat the end of the thread in nail varnish, and then allow it to set.

Mrs E Bostock, Northwich, Cheshire

27

To make it easier to pass the thread through the eye of the needle, try doubling the end.

Mrs M Lockett, Burton-by-Tarporley, Cheshire

To thread a needle easily, spray the end of the cotton with hairspray, and let it dry.

Mrs E Williams, Hull, Humberside

If you have difficulty threading a needle, place it in front of a white background: the eye will seem larger.

C M H Goodman, Windsor, Berkshire

If poor eyesight makes threading a needle difficult, get someone else to thread several needles on to a couple of reels of cotton. You can then cut off one at a time, sliding the rest along the thread for future use.

Mrs M Moran, High Peak

To remove rust from needles, place them on a smooth concrete, or brick, surface, and rub them to and fro with your shod foot.

Mrs F Brojer, Maidenhead, Berkshire

To sharpen blunt sewing needles, sew through emery paper.

Mrs M A Carter, Colchester, Essex

Prevent reels of cotton from unravelling in the workbox by securing the end of the thread with a small piece of sticky tape.

M Hubling, Ashford, Kent

ಬಿ

To prevent damage to your dishwasher, and to other items in the machine, cover the points of sharp knives with a wine cork before placing them in the cutlery basket.

P M Sheridan, Tunbridge Wells, Kent

Don't oil door hinges that squeak or repair floorboards that creak. They warn you of unwanted intruders during the night!

Mrs M Cooper, Manchester

Do not place knives in the drainer point upwards: apart from the risk of lacerating your wrists when retrieving them, ivory and bone handles will deteriorate more quickly if water is allowed to run down them.

Katherine Douglas, Gloucester

If a fat fire starts in your frying-pan, use baking soda to smother the flames – never water, which causes the flames to explode into a ball of fire.

S Whittle, Banbury, Oxon

If you live on your own, check that the back door is locked before answering the front door. Burglars work in pairs.

Mrs J Knight, Reading, Berkshhire

Place a small mirror on the inside wall by your front door so that you can see who's at the door before opening it fully.

A K Smith, Coulsdon, Surrey

&

If you find it difficult to open the new ring-pull cans, use the handle of a wooden spoon as a lever.
B Gandy, Farnham, Surrey

When opening a tin with a can-opener, slow down as you reach the end. The lid will then twist up towards you, saving you from having to fish about for it.

Carolyn Whitehead, Yatton, Somerset

Put a rubber band around a measuring jug: you can then use it as a marker to underline the appropriate measurement, making it easier to read accurately.

Miss M Hume, Stalybridge, Cheshire

If you are shortsighted, mark the 9 on the telephone dial with bright-red paint – easy to distinguish without spectacles in an emergency.

Joy Bell, Bury St Edmunds, Suffolk

If you ever need to use the phone in the dark – perhaps to make an emergency call – remember that on most push-button phones there is a small pimple on the number 5 button, making it easy to locate the other numbers.

Angela Bennett, London

If you cannot see something you have dropped on the floor, lie down on your front and look along the floor's surface. You will see the object standing out.

Joan Hill, Harwell, Oxon

For a hearing-impaired relative, fix a timer to a bedside lamp to act as an alarm clock.

Sheila Smith, Coulsdon, Surrey

To ensure that you will recall something occurring to you just before falling asleep, drop something from the bedside table to the floor.

Mrs J Seed, Nelson, Lancashire

ଚୠ

Turn rubber gloves inside out and they will slide on and off your hands more easily.

Mrs I Straw, Retford, Nottinghamshire

Keep talcum powder by the sink to sprinkle into rubber gloves and they will last three times longer than usual.

Penelope Bourgeois, Rustington, West Sussex

Use bicycle-clips to secure rolled-up sleeves when washing up.

Hannah Balfour, London

Before starting a dirty or greasy job, coat your hands in washing-up liquid. When you have finished, the dirt will simply rinse off.

W D Murgatroyd, Cwymbran, Gwent

To make your oven-gloves easier to access in a hurry, sew a strong magnet inside them and then stick them to the cookers.

Mrs Walker, Deal, Kent

To avoid oversleeping, place your alarm clock on a tin tray – it will make a lot more noise.

Mrs J Spry, New Quay, Ceredigion

When filling a new hotwater bottle, add a few drops of glycerine: it will make the rubber more flexible and stop it perishing.

Mrs J Sim, Gatcombe, Isle of Wight

∞

Wipe lightbulbs with vanilla extract or perfume. When the light is turned on, the heat created will cause the scent to be released.

Sheila Smith, Coulsdon, Surrey

Try spraying perfume onto your vacuum-cleaner bag to fragrance your room.

Jennie Wolfe, Retford, Nottinghamshire

An apple-scented candle will eliminate the odour of tobacco.

Claudia Parkinson, Oxford

Keep the paper perfume and aftershave samples that are often given away in magazines, and place them on hot radiators. Result: a sweetly scented room for free.

Heather Marks, Biddenham, Bedforshire

Don't throw away old pot-pourri: wrap it in a piece of muslin, secured with string or ribbon, and then place it in your clothes' drawers or linen cupboard.

Ursula Sargeson, Marlborough, Wiltshire

To keep your fridge smelling fresh, slice a lemon in half and stand it on the top shelf.

Shirley Van der Beek, Wraysbury, Berkshire

An inch of cat-litter in the bottom of a kitchen bin keeps the bin smelling fresh and soaks up leaks from split bags.

C McKillop, Kingsbridge, Devon

To keep your sceptic tank efficient and sweet-smelling, wash four ounces of bicarbonate of soda down the kitchen sink every fourteen days.

Janet Gould, Trehan, Cornwall

80

Silence squeaky floorboards or stairs with a good shake of talcum powder in the joists or gaps between them.

Mrs J Roberts, Enfield Wash, Middlesex

To remove candle grease from carpets, cover the affected area with kitchen towels and press with a hot iron until the towels have absorbed the wax and the carpet is clean.

Mrs C Murray, Thurso, Caithness

A small burn on the carpet can be removed by rubbing the area with a raw potato.

Angela Pavry, Colchester, Essex

Treat cigarette burns in carpets by rubbing them with the edge of a silver coin.

J Dyke, Horsham, West Sussex

To remove red-wine stains from a carpet, cover the area immediately with salt. Once it is dry, vacuum it up.

Kathy Corteen, Orpington, Kent

When cleaning stains from carpet, upholstery and clothes, use your hairdryer to speed drying.

Mrs E Campbell, Bexhill, East Sussex

Try wearing damp rubber gloves to de-fluff carpet in awkward corners and on stairs.

Paula Wood, Wivelsfield, East Sussex

To clean a doormat without creating dust everywhere, put the mat in a bin-liner, and then shake it vigorously.

Richard Straw, Grantham, Lincolnshire

To clean your rug this winter, leave it face down on newly fallen snow for a while before shaking it. Dirt will be left behind in the snow.

Miss Sandra Ford, Sevenoaks, Kent

ഈ

When taking down curtains for cleaning, mark the position of the curtain-hooks on the heading tape. This saves time when rehanging them.

Olive Jeram, Newquay, Cornwall

Use old curtains to interline your new ones. It's cheap and works beautifully.

Hilary Derouet, Canterbury, Kent

To ensure curtain-rails run smoothly, rub them occasionally with some furniture polish.

Mrs Helen Wren, Boston, Lincolnshire

Don't throw out old shower curtains. Use them as picnic tablecloths, temporary curtains, furniture-covers when decorating, capes for wearing while having your hair cut, and cupboard linings.

E Wilson, Birmingham, West Midlands

To avoid the need to iron net curtains, fold them neatly before putting them in the washing machine. Wash and rinse; then immediately remove them from the machine and drip-dry.

Felicity Smith, Swindon, Wiltshire

સ૭

To avoid losing your grip when moving furniture, wear rubber gloves .

Miss J Butler, West Molesey, Surrey

To take some of the backache out of shifting a heavy or awkward-shaped object, lever it onto a skateboard.

Jane Ash, Preston, Lancashire

When moving heavy objects across a hard floor surface, such as tiles, put a mixture of washing-up liquid and water on the floor immediately in front of the object, and it will glide along effortlessly.

Geraldine Dyke, Birmingham, West Midlands

Place a rectangle of carpet, tuft-side down, under each of your heavy kitchen appliances, and they will be easy to move when you need to clean them or pull them out for repair.

Irene Starr, Carryduff, Co Down

સ૭

If your car-wash sponge absorbs so much detergent that it won't rinse out, rub the sponge lightly with ordinary soap, and then rinse. Magic!

E MacSween, Inverness

Let rain take the strain from car washing. Apply car shampoo if heavy rain is imminent, and no rinsing will be necessary.

Mrs D Berry, Tarporley, Cheshire

To remove hardened bird-lime without damaging your car's paintwork: cover it with newspaper, and then soak with boiling water. When cool, simply wipe off.

Nigel Trapp, Bournemouth, Dorset

Apply clear nail varnish on and around chips on car windscreens, inside and out, to prevent them from turning into major cracks.

R K Bobal, Poole, Dorset

When replying to car adverts, ask if the car is still available. If the answer is 'What car?' you are talking to a dealer.

M Grummell, Kettering, Northamptonshire

If you are not going to use your bicycle for some time, store it upside down to prevent the tyres from splitting.

Mrs C Tulett, Sidmouth, Devon

℘

When packing breakable items – either for storage, or for sending through the post – wrap each item in damp newspaper: it will dry to a protective shell.

Mrs J M Chohan, Machynlleth, Powys

To give yourself extra kitchen storage space, re-move the kick-board beneath your kitchen cupboards, screw it to the front of one of the large, strong mushroom trays from the supermarket, and add a knob to the front.

Pauline Kelly, Longfield, Kent

To store plastic bags, make a sleeve out of fabric. Hem the top to take a hanging cord, and elasticate the bottom to contain the bags. Hang from a peg. Push carrier bags in through the top, and retrieve them from the bottom.

Barbara Cartwright, Burnham-on-Sea, Somerset

Cut off the bottom three inches of empty plastic milk-bottles, then place them in your kitchen cupboards and stand any bottles of oil, vinegar or sauce in them – no more sticky shelves.

B Semple, Ottery St Mary, Devon

Small spares and accessories can be kept safely together, along with the instructions and guarantee, in a zip-fastening, labelled freezer bag.

Philip Irwin, Peterborough, Cambridgeshire

The resealable mesh bags supplied with dishwasher tablets make useful containers for small items.

E Scott, Hatfield, Hertfordshire

Disused lever-type door handles make very good heavy-duty hooks for garage or workshop.

V Hitchman, Ilfracombe, Devon

&

To make them less bulky in the bin-bag, soften empty boxes in water and tear them into pieces.

Christine Manton, Kirkham, Lancashire

So that they take up less space in your dustbin, squeeze air out of empty plastic bottles and then screw the top back on tight.

G J Andrews, London

ဢ

To prevent wax running down a candle, sprinkle a pinch of salt on it before lighting.

R D Bingham, Romsey, Hampshire

When carrying a cup of tea or coffee, put a spoon in the cup and you won't spill any.

Sue Jones, Brighton, East Sussex

ဢ

To restore table-mats that have become tatty, paste on a picture from a calendar or magazine, and then seal with a coat of heat-resistant varnish.

Mrs J Shone, Whitely Bay, Tyne & Wear

Dinner plates to heat? Short of oven space? Plunge them into a washing-up bowl filled with hot water.

Mrs Mary Leeland, Chelmsford, Essex

Place a dinner plate under food heating in the microwave. Spillages are contained, and the risk of burning your fingers is greatly reduced.

Mrs U Luton, Saffron Walden, Essex

&

Before storing hotwater bottles, fill them with half a pint of water before laying them flat. This will prevent the interior rubber sides from sticking to each other.

Miss J Blackley, Cookstown, Co Tyrone

&

And some wisdoms from the very boundaries of common sense ...

To rid your property of seagulls and pigeons, put up a plastic owl.

Stella Walton, Torquay, Devon

Rather than spend extra money on printed-paper kitchen towels, buy the cheaper, white ones, and paint them yourself.

J Pearson, London

Children

If you haven't a suitable tablecloth for a children's party, you can use large sheets of tin-foil.

Kate Alder, Oxted, Surrey

When you are having children to stay, protect your dining table at meal-times with an old duvet cover instead of a tablecloth.

Mrs Diane R Young, Luton, Bedfordshire

When teaching a child to use chopsticks, select wooden ones as they grip the food better than other types. To help keep the sticks in the same position in the hand, knot the tops together with a fine, two-and-a-half-inch elastic band.

Miss Emily E M Shaw-Hardie

To make it easier for children to eat spaghetti with a spoon, use scissors to chop it up in the pan before heating.

Miss M Wilson, Sheffield

ℰℑ

To get further use from children's leggings when they wear at the knee, cut them above the knee, and hem to make cycling shorts.

Mrs J P Morris, Doncaster, South Yorkshire

Lengthen the life of crawling children's trousers by sewing soft shoulder-pads inside at knee level. They prevent sore knees, too.

D R Andrew, Audlem, Cheshire

To clean an old teddy, place it in a plastic bag, rub a sprinkling of cornflour into it with your fingers, leave for several hours, and then brush off.

Patricia Laing, Mold, Flintshire

&

Draw a smiley face on the instep of children's shoes or wellies: smiles together means shoes will always be on the correct feet!

Doreen Mitchell, Brentwood, Essex

To prevent children losing their shoelaces, thread the laces through the holes using the crossover method, and put a few stitches in the first cross-over to secure the lace.

Caroline Gilbert, Kingswells, Aberdeen

Wet children's shoelaces before tying – that way they won't come unfastened.

J D Pilling, Rossendale, Lancashire

&

To ensure that buttons are in the correct holes, teach children to button up cardigans or coats from the bottom.

Mrs J Miller, Esher, Surrey

Teach young children to push their scarves and hats into their coat-sleeves to help prevent loss in the school cloakroom.

Mrs R Vowles, Lytham St Annes, Lancashire

To keep identically coloured school socks in their original pairs (and so avoid having to match up slightly different sizes after each wash), colour code the pairs with coloured thread sewn into the inside of the elastic tops.

Elizabeth Shaw, London

શ

To keep young visitors busy, help them make their own skittles game: half fill empty washing-up liquid bottles with gravel, seal tightly, and then paint.

Alice Coffey, Stockport, Cheshire

A roll of white wallpaper-lining paper provides a cheap and generous supply of drawing paper.

Mrs R Coote, Iver, Buckinghamshire

Apply a light coating of hairspray over a child's drawing to prevent the colours from fading and rubbing off, and to strengthen the paper.

Kirsty Currie, Newton Stewart, Dumfries

Use resealable plastic foodpacks for storing children's felt-tip pens.

D Hancock, Totland, Isle of Wight

43

To store a child's snooker table, place a skateboard under either end and simply slide it under a bed.

Mrs C M Naylor, St Helens, Merseyside

∞

Store packs of wet-wipes upside down to keep the top ones moist.

Mrs Sandra Payne, Meopham, Kent

A folded sheet of plastic bubble-wrap makes an ideal, disposable changing-mat, which is especially useful when travelling.

Irene Pitt, Potters Bar, Hertfordshire

Put young children's car-booster seats on cinema or theatre seats to raise them up and so provide them with a better view.

Mary Priest, Kidderminster, Worcestershire

∞

When photographing a young child, a thoughtful pose is achieved by screwing up a length of sticky tape and placing it in the palm of his or her hand.

Jennifer Bromley, North Shoebury, Essex

When photographing your baby, first photograph a white card showing the date: if there is a long delay before the pictures are developed, you will know precisely when they were taken.

Patricia Hardie, London

∞

Help children learn to read – put the subtitles on when they watch television.

Ron Mayers, Exeter, Devon

To teach children to distinguish left from right, ask them to hold out their hands with palms down. The thumb and index finger of the left hand form an L.

L Major, Cleckheaton, West Yorkshire

Offer a reward to the child who picks up the last toy or piece of Lego – clearing up will become fun.

Margaret Igglesden, London

To remove a child's armbands painlessly after a swimming lesson, take them off while he or she is still in the water: they will slip off easily.

Rachel Lawrence, Bristol, Somerset

ॐ

For safety when bathing children, place a bath-towel over the taps.

J Edward, Rugby, Warwickshire

Tie the handles of cupboards together with loops of strong elastic to keep curious children out.

Jill Griffiths, Stoke Fleming, South Devon

Plastic trellis makes effective covering for sandpits. It discourages cats and dogs, yet is light enough for children to remove by themselves.

Mrs Harding, Huntingdon, Cambridgeshire

Be prepared for those occasions when you can't make it to collect your children from school: have a simple family password to enable your child to identify the adult that you send in your place.

John Miles, Rugby, Warwickshire

Christmas

For an unusual table centrepiece, spray gold or silver glitter on the shells of a bowlful of mixed nuts.

Mrs Diana Irwin, Belfast

Abandoned plastic hub-caps make good supports for wreaths – especially those with slots through which to thread holly, etc.

J Pattison, Bristol, Somerset

For lasting evergreen decorations, wrap a raw potato in foil, insert a skewer to hang it up, and poke holly and other greenery into it. Decorate with ribbon and baubles.

Cynthia Fisher, Brundall, Norfolk

&

To keep a holly wreath secure on a loved one's grave during winter gales, cut a coat-hanger in half vertically, and use the resulting U-shaped pieces as pegs to pin it into the ground.

R Harrison, Leyland, Lancashire

Dip balloons in warm water before blowing them up – it makes it easier.

A Hodson, Lawford Dale, Essex

&

Any unwanted or broken pieces of jewellery can be recycled into interesting decorations for your Christmas tree.

K Giddings, Preston, Lancashire

Stand the Christmas tree in a bucket filled with unpeeled potatoes. It will remain upright, and the moisture will help prevent the tree from shedding its needles.

Pam Kilbane, Ivybridge, Devon

Brighten up your faded Christmas lights with glass-paints obtainable from your local art shop. You can use the same paints to create coloured lights from simple white or transparent ones.

Linda Evans, Upminster, Essex

Hang bells or some other noisy decoration on the lower branches of the Christmas tree to warn you when children or pets are near it.

Miss E K Marriott, Hinckley, Leicestershire

Save Christmas holly decorations. When dry, place them in flower borders to deter cats.

W A Kennett, Dover, Kent

ɛꙩ

Turn tiny gifts for adults and children into snow-ball surprises. Cover the gift in cotton wool and add a coloured bow.

Mrs I Boden, Wilmslow, Cheshire

To save fumbling about in the dark when filling a Christmas stocking, take two identical stockings, fill one, then swap it for the empty one in the child's room.

Claire Walker, Normandy, Surrey

ɛꙩ

Use the thinnest paper for wrapping presents for very small children. It's easier for little hands to rip open.

Pam Chadwick, Lechlade, Gloucestershire

Use paper Christmas tablecloths for wrapping extra large presents.

Mrs E Fisher, Corsham, Wiltshire

Make a list of the senders of your Christmas cards to save having to trawl through address books to compile a list the following year.

Jane Ash, Preston, Lancashire

ಬ

Take photographs of your children opening their presents from relatives, and then enclose the prints with their thank-you letters.

Madeleine Wright, Leicester

ಬ

To stop saucepans turning black when steaming Christmas puddings, add vinegar or apple-peelings to the water.

Irene Ainsworth, Chippenham, Wiltshire

To get a good flame on your Christmas pudding, sprinkle it with one heaped tablespoon of sugar, add spirit, and light.

Mrs M D Lintin, Salisbury, Wiltshire

Layer left-over Christmas pudding with buttered bread. Add an egg-custard made from two eggs mixed with half a pint of milk, and bake till set and golden brown. Delicious!

Mrs Ann Gwyther, Llandaff, Cardiff

When you've eaten the Christmas pudding, save the plastic bowl it came in and use it as a container for microwaving other foods.

Sarah Parkinson, Stroud, Gloucestershire

ॐ

To facilitate easy removal of the turkey from the roasting tin: before roasting, place the turkey in a home-made string cradle and then into the tin, leaving four of the cradle's strings hanging over each side. When the bird is cooked, simply grasp the strings and lift.

Mrs D Rogers, Newcastle upon Tyne

Turkey breasts will stay more moist if the bird is cooked breast-down for the first half hour.

C Medcalf, Rickmansworth, Hertfordshire

ॐ

When roasting chestnuts, make a slit in the side of all except one. This will pop when cooked, indicating that the others are also ready.

Mrs A Billimoria, London

When making brandy butter, warm the brandy to blood heat: the fat will not curdle, and it will take extra brandy if needed.

Mrs D S Dunford, Wareham, Dorset

To give the ideal sherry trifle its taste, whisk the sherry into the thick cream, adding only a little to the sponge base.

B Percy, Egham, Surrey

೮つ

To ease the bloated feeling after Christmas dinner: chew a few thin slices of ginger in syrup.

Mrs M Owen, Calverton, Nottinghamshire

೮つ

To retain the sparkle on gold and silver Christmas decorations, wrap them in aluminium foil before packing them away.

J Carrier, Codsall, South Staffordshire

Empty egg-cartons make ideal protective packaging for storing delicate Christmas baubles, etc.

Mrs Gill Kelly, Bognor Regis, West Sussex

After using special silver or silver-plated items at Christmas, wrap them in clingfilm before storing. They will emerge tarnish free.

Jenny Selby-Green, Chipping Norton, Oxon

To remove glitter and tinsel from furniture and carpets, wrap a length of sticky tape (adhesive-side up) around two fingers, and dab off.

Ian Davidson, Billericay, Essex

❦

On New Year's Day, save yourself the inconvenience caused by making out wrongly dated cheques by writing the new year in the date section of the next few cheques in your chequebook.

Mrs G R Smith, Nottingham

❦

And some wisdoms from the very boundaries of common sense ...

To make the most of the Christmas-time big-screen action on a small-screen television, watch through binoculars.

J Stewart, Ilkley, West Yorkshire

For a stress-free Christmas, invite all your relations to stay with you for the week. The day before they arrive, book yourself into a hotel and remain there for the duration.

Sarah Richardson, Carlisle, Cumbria

Clothing & Accessories

Supermarket baby-wipes will remove most food- and grease-stains from clothes (even silk) if used immediately.

V Stirzaker, East Allington, South Devon

To remove grease from clothing, sprinkle talcum powder over it. A few hours later, simply brush it away.

Deborah Mann, Sutton Coldfield, West Midlands

To remove paint from clothing, allow the paint to dry and then smear butter over the stain. Scrub with a firm brush, rinse, and then wash on the usual machine cycle.

Ben King, Saffron Walden, Essex

Ink-stains on clothes can be removed with lemon juice.

Mrs J Smith, Stockport, Hampshire

To remove biro-marks from clothes, leather suites, etc, dab with household antiseptic.

Mrs L G White, Oldham, Lancashire

To remove blood from clothes, linen or cottons, soak the stain in milk before washing.

Eithne McCormack, Liverpool

To get rid of fruit-stains on cotton or polyester, dab with neat bleach and immediately plunge into cold water.

Anon

To remove beetroot-stains from garments, apply milk to the stained area before washing.

Mrs G Payne, Birmingham, West Midlands

To remove creosote from clothes, soak the affected area with nail-varnish remover, then wash as normal. Since more than one treatment and rewash may be necessary, do not include fabric-softener in the final rinse until the stain has disappeared.

Sarah Richardson, Carlisle, Cumbria

To remove stains from clothing, cover them with oil of eucalyptus and dust liberally with french chalk. Allow to dry completely, and then brush off.

Mrs E M Fisher, Hockley, Essex

To remove stuck-on chewing gum, smother with peanut butter and wash as normal. Works on fabric, carpet, shoes, skin, and hair.

Carol Edwards, Northampton

To get rid of scorch-marks on cotton or linen materials, rub with raw onion before washing.

Mrs A Oliver, Newcastle upon Tyne

ೞ

If you've spent time in a smoky atmosphere, you can rid your clothes of the smell by hanging them over a warm radiator.

Barbara Masters, Stockport, Cheshire

When a baby has been sick on clothes or blankets, a solution of bicarbonate of soda and water applied to the area will take away the smell.

Mrs P M Davis, Tewkesbury, Gloucestershire

ଈଠ

Keep florists wrapping paper for lining drawers.

Trudie Leibling, London

If you haven't drawer or cupboard space for your hairdryer, place it in a carrier bag, and then hang it on a coat-hanger in the wardrobe.

Miss J E Stiles, Birmingham, West Midlands

Keep your make-up and jewellery organised by storing it in one of the compartment-boxes designed for nails and screws, etc.

Judith Jones, Chorlton, Manchester

ଈଠ

To remove scratches from glass watch-faces, rub with a small piece of silver polish wadding.

Pam Chadwick, Lechlade, Gloucestershire

Make an old wind-up watch work again by placing it in the deep freeze inside a plastic bag. The thawed ice will dislodge the dust.

Mrs P B Prabhu, London

ଈଠ

Use cola to clean gold. Test a small area first, then immerse the item fully to remove tarnish.

B Thompson, Hythe, Kent

A teaspoon of bicarbonate of soda mixed with a little cold water makes an effective and inexpensive cleaner for diamonds.

Mrs C E Greville, Ware, Hertfordshire

To clean intricate or deeply grooved pieces of silver jewellery, apply toothpaste with a soft-bristled brush and rinse off. Once dry, polish to a shine with a dry toothbrush.

Kate Alldis, Marlborough, Wiltshire

 හ

Quick clean for dirty spectacles: wipe with neat vodka.

Mrs G Thompson, Stoke, Staffordshire

To prevent small screws from coming loose in spectacles, tighten the screws and then paint them with clear nail varnish.

Hazel Williams, Wedmore, Somerset

Old pencil-cases make great cases for spectacles.

Miss A C Davies, Builth Wells, Powys

To find a lost contact-lens, cover the vacuum-cleaner nozzle with a pair of tights, and slowly sweep the area.

Michael Dodds, Glasgow

If you drop a contact-lens into a bowl of water or onto the floor, shine a powerful torch over the area. The lens will concentrate the light into a bright, visible spot.

Mrs M Lloyd, Ellesmere, Shropshire

 හ

The cartridges from wine-bottle boxes are ideal for storing and organizing shoes in the bottom of the wardrobe.

Mrs G Kershaw, Hebden Bridge, West Yorkshire

Always polish new shoes before wearing them. It keeps them clean, good looking and long lasting.

Anon

Use hairspray to polish shoes – it's quicker and cheaper than shoe polish, and never fails to give a long-lasting shine.

Mrs W M Woolman, Leicester

The inside of a banana-skin is a good shoe cleaner.

Katherine Douglas, Gloucester

For an exceptionally deep shine, leave shoe polish on your shoes overnight, and then brush up the following morning.

Emily L Mallard, Cirencester, Gloucestershire

Use spray paint in metallic or fluorescent colours to give cheeky new life to old shoes, boots and jackets made from synthetic materials.

Miss B Dorf, London

Restore old suede shoes by holding them over the steam from the kettle.

K Giddings, Preston, Lancashire

છ૭

Before you pull your waterproof trousers on over your boots, cover the boots with plastic bags – no mud on the inside.

G Stone, Altrincham, Cheshire

To mend a leaky wellington boot, solder the edges together with a red-hot poker or skewer.

Mrs J Wright, Tavistock, Devon

Cut a pair of old wellington boots down to the ankle. They make good slip-ons for the garden.

Mrs K M Wren, Salisbury, Wiltshire

To dry out damp wellington boots or shoes, stuff the insides with newspaper.

Elizabeth Clarke, Diss, Norfolk

To make canvas shoes completely waterproof, spray them with tent-waterproofing solution, obtainable from any camping shop.

Miss D Davidson, Teignmouth, Devon

ॐ

To soften and stretch leather shoes, stuff them with paper and leave them overnight in the freezer.

D Fulford, London

Beware of wasps hibernating in your footwear.

Mrs K L White, Bury St Edmunds, Suffolk

ॐ

When shortening a skirt or dress for yourself, you can check that the hem is even by wearing the skirt over a white night-dress when you stand before the mirror.

Mrs E Martin, London

To keep a new zip in position while sewing it into a garment, arrange it in place first with sticky tape, and then sew through the tape. Once the zip is secure, the tape can be gently removed.

Miss E M L Hyatt OBE, York

To hide snagged threads in clothes, push a darning needle halfway through the fabric next to the snag; feed the offending thread through the eye of the needle, and pull through out of sight.

Bob Sharpe, Welwyn Garden City, Hertfordshire

To prevent fraying of trouser hems, sew a small button about half an inch from the edge of the hem near the crease on the inside of each leg.

F Humphreys, Formby, Merseyside

ॐ

If you have a very hairy chest, wear your vest backwards – the higher back section will cover more of the hair and make your shirts look whiter.

Leonard Cumming, Rothesay, Strathclyde

To change dress without soiling garments or ruining make-up, wear a shower-cap.

Megan McConnachie, Newport, Pembrokeshire

Getting into a wetsuit is much easier if you put plastic bags over your feet.

Dr S E Halliday, London

When pregnant, don't waste your money on expensive maternity tights. Instead, wear extra-large tights back to front.

Kathryn King, Bristol, Somerset

To remove sheer tights from less than perfectly smooth heels, rub in a little handcream before gently peeling them off. No snags.

Mrs M A Webster, Groby, Leicestershire

∾

If you suspect that a garment is harbouring moth larvae, you can ensure that they are destroyed by placing the item in a plastic bag and leaving it in the freezer for twenty-four hours.

Mrs B Tracken, London

To prevent moths getting at clothes, place some conkers in one or two small dishes in wardrobes and cupboards.

Mrs Irene Eade, East Barnet, Hertfordshire

To discourage moths, stuff newspaper into the sleeves and pockets of your hanging garments.

Mrs Pat Godleman, Ashford, Kent

Keep pillows fresh and dust-mite free by putting them in a tumble-dryer for twenty minutes.

Mrs E Morgan, West Turville, Buckinghamshire

∾

When hanging skirts by their waist-tabs, turn the skirt inside-out first to prevent the waistband folding over and creasing.

Mrs J J Wolgan, Johnstone, Renfrewshire

Pin unwanted shoulder-pads to the ends of coat-hangers to prevent soft garments from stretching.

Mrs J F Ball, Hull, East Yorkshire

Stop shoulder-bags from slipping off the shoulder by attaching a piece of adhesive-backed Velcro to the underside of the strap. The hooks in the Velcro will cling to your clothes.

Mrs A M Carfoot, Fulfood, York

To prevent trouser zips sliding down, fix a keyring to the zip's tab, hook the ring over the waistband button, and fasten the button.

Catherine Lacey, Devizes, Wiltshire

A kitchen-roll slit lengthways and slipped over a the trouser-bar of a coat-hanger will prevent unwanted creases in stored trousers.

Lynne McQuade, Barrow-in-Furness, Cumbria

Stop your dress or skirt from clinging to tights by spraying the tights (after putting them on) with a light mist of hairspray.

Mrs J Coals, Budleigh Salterton, Devon

Prevent the neckline of a garment from yellowing during storage by arranging folded handkerchiefs around it before enclosing the whole garment in plastic.

Miss P Stacke, London

Stop sheets from wrapping themselves around clothes-lines on breezy days by pegging both edges of the sheet to the line and placing a long bamboo cane in the fold.

A Ealand, Redcar, Cleveland

ഇ

Starched tights won't snag so easily.

Mrs Joan Mead, Northampton

Stop a ladder in your tights from running further by dabbing the area with soap.

J Swindin, Ipswich, Suffolk

Thoroughly wet new nylon tights and stockings and place in a container and freeze. Thaw and dry carefully, and they will last much longer.

Mrs B Greenshields, Bognor Regis, West Sussex

ഇ

Buttons will not come off so easily if you dab the threads of the button with clear nail varnish after sewing them on.

Sheila Smith, Coulsdon, Surrey

When sewing on buttons, coat the thread in beeswax and they will remain in place for years.

Mrs L P Holliday, Frimley, Surrey

If a button comes off, straighten a paper-clip and pass each end through a hole in the button. Push ends into the fabric, and secure behind for a quick repair job.

John Roger, Hereford

∞

Marks left by pegs on shoulders of garments can be flattened out by rubbing them with a damp cloth.

Ms C McManus, Weymouth, Dorset

Soak new wooden clothes-pegs for twenty-four hours before use to prevent them from leaving dirty marks on your clothes.

Mrs L Bowring, Stoney Stratton, Somerset

To prevent pegs marking knitted garments on the clothes-line, thread the leg of an old pair of tights through each sleeve, and (for extra security) the waistband of the tights through the neck; then peg the feet (and waistband) to the line.

Mrs L Jones, Worcester

∞

Rub soap along the inside of trouser-creases, then press as usual to get a really clean, sharp crease.

John Roger, Hereford

To avoid having to iron cotton sheets and pillow-cases, place them folded into the washing machine, and then refold them before putting them straight into the airing cupboard.

Mrs M Lloyd, Telford, Shropshire

To save having to iron a shirt, hang it up and spray it with water. The creases will fall out as the shirt dries.

J Cater, Nottingham

When faced with a large amount of ironing to do, spread the largest, flat item (such as a tablecloth) on the ironing-board first, then pressing smaller items over it. It will then need less ironing itself.

Mrs M Cooke, Maidstone, Kent

If you put washed shirts on a hanger as soon as they are taken out of the washing machine, they will need little or no ironing.

Mrs F Holbrook, Welwyn Garden City, Hertfordshire

To save time and effort, place items for pressing under your mattress overnight. Your body heat and weight does the pressing.

R A Smith, London

When pressing woollens, place the garment under newspaper and press as usual. (There is sufficient dampness in the newspaper to negate the need for any additional water.)

Mrs J M Wagstaff, Rugby, Warwickshire

∞

If you have run out of starch, dip garments in water in which pasta or rice has been cooked. Iron whilst damp.

Mrs J A Bristow, Littlehampton

∞

Fasten bra-hooks before putting them into the washing machine to prevent them catching on to other clothes.

Freda Gibson, London

An easy way to machine-wash tights, delicate underwear, and small items that may snag themselves on other clothes, is to put each item in an empty washing-tablet net, and then wash with the usual load.

Mrs Karen Brown, Herne Hill, London

To remove the excess water from delicate underwear or tights, don't use the washing-machine spin cycle; try a salad spinner.

Mrs Patricia Andrews, Huddersfield, Yorkshire

Save the ends of toilet soap, and place them in a small bag made out of old tights by knotting each end. Use for washing underwear.

Eileen Caren, Preston, Lancashire

∽

To stop woollen garments from shrinking, soak them in cold water for a few hours until all the fibres are saturated, and then wash as usual.

Sybil Bleach, Lytham St Annes, Lancashire

Roll handwashed clothes in a towel to remove excess water and so prevent them from dripping on the floor when you hang them up.

Mrs Maxwell-Irving, Stirling

To keep track of stains when handwashing a garment, thread a piece of coloured cotton through each one. When you pre-wash – and the material darkens as it is immersed in the water – you will still be able to locate the marks.

Margaret Fearn, Coalville, Leicestershire

Handwashing with shampoo and conditioner gives old woollies a new lease of life.

Mrs G H Smith, Salisbury, Wiltshire

To soften hard water for handwashing clothes, add bicarbonate of soda to the water.

Jane Ash, Preston, Lancashire

∽

Wash and dry navy or black garments inside out to prevent them from fading and bobbling.

Mrs B J Emmett, Cheddar, Somerset

Always include a towel with every washing load.
The texture helps to clean the other items.

Mrs J Coleman, Stanford, Lincolnshire

Gently hold airing laundry against your lips. If it
stays cold it's not properly dry; if it warms immediately it's ready to wear or use.

Mrs J P Waters, Haywards Heath, Sussex

To save a lot of time spent in sorting your clothes
into separate loads prior to washing, invest in two
wicker clothes-storage baskets: a dark one for
coloured clothes, and a light one for whites.

Elizabeth Shaw, London

ം

When hanging out your washing, give each item a
firm shake before pegging it onto the washing-
line. This will remove most of the creases, and so
reduce ironing time considerably.

Mary Wilmot, Sunbury on Thames, Middlesex

In winter, hang washing in the greenhouse to prevent it from being soaked in the event of a sudden
rain shower.

Joy Bell, Bury St Edmunds, Suffolk

Bofre hanging out your shirts to dry, place them
on a coat-hanger, and button the neck, before
pegging the hanger (not the shirt) to the clothes-
line. If there isn't time to iron them when they are
dry you can immediately transfer them to the
wardrobe and so save space in your ironing basket.

Irene Pitt, Potters Bar, Hertfordshire

To enable you to bring washing inside quickly when it rains, peg small items, (socks, and so on) onto a plastic coat-hanger, and then suspend this securely from the washing-line.

Brenda Hughes, Congleton, Cheshire

For easy access to the pegs when hanging out your washing, keep them permanently in an apron with a large pocket at the front.

Mrs C Buckell, Hemel Hempstead, Hertfordshire

ဆော

Don't throw out pyjamas that have gone at the knees; cut the worn section away, and hem the remainder to make trendy shorts for the warmer weather.

Mrs Margaret Smith, Dundee

To make silk clothing look like new, roll, place in the freezer while damp, then iron.

Mrs M Joyce, East Wittering, West Sussex

಄

And some wisdoms from the very boundaries of common sense ...

In an emergency, clean date-stones can be used as replacement duffle-coat toggles.

J Whelan, Salisbury, Wiltshire

Life's too short for washing tights: paint your legs instead.

Frances Wilder, London

To clean a gold ring, bury it in the garden for twenty-four hours, then rinse and polish with a soft cloth.

D Barnham, London

DIY

When spraying small items with metallic aerosol paints, prevent damage to the surrounding area by placing the items in a large, open, cardboard box.

Jane Booth, Andover, Hampshire

When painting skirting boards, first put masking tape along the edge of the carpet to catch any paint-runs or drips.

Harry Barnes, Tunbridge Wells, Kent

Protect a door while painting around it by covering it with an old fitted sheet – the elastic will hold it in place.

Mrs M Coates, Wigton, Cumbria

To prevent emulsion from spattering your spectacles when you are roller-painting a ceiling, stretch clingfilm over your lenses.

J W Dawn, Littleover, Derbyshire

Use a disposable, plastic shower-cap as protective headgear when painting ceilings.

Claudia Parkinson

To prevent paint from running down your arm when painting a ceiling, make a large collar for the brush by piercing a hole in a paper plate and pushing the brush's handle through it.

Susan Webster, Derby

∽

When using a small tin of paint, place it in a larger, empty tin with a handle so that you can rest your brushes alongside it.

Valerie Galler, Gravesend, Kent

Rather than using the side of the paint-tin to wipe your brush, use a piece of string tied between the bases of the tin's handle.

Mr and Mrs Davies, Chichester, West Sussex

Don't use metallic paint on radiators. It tends to absorb heat rather than allowing it to escape into the room.

Patricia Hardie, London

Before painting, apply moisturising lotion to your hands. Any paint-splashes will easily wash off when the job is done.

J Rippon, London

To shut newly painted windows before the paint is completely dry, insert wax paper from cereal packets between window and frame.

I E Howell, Arundel, West Sussex

To remove paint-splashes from windows, rub with hot vinegar.

Mrs P J Hatton, Stroud, Gloucestershire

℘

If you are painting from a ladder using a paint-pot that doesn't have a handle, place the pot in a bucket, and suspend the bucket from ladder with wire or a butcher's hook.

David Price, Marlborough, Wiltshire

When working from a ladder, carry your nails in a bum-bag to save having to climb down every time you need one.

Ms A Shell, Alnwick, Northumberland

Stop the legs of ladders sinking into soft earth or turf by fitting empty tins over the legs.

Leslie Baverstock, Hartbury, Gloucestershire

Spring decorating? Collect the stackable (usually fruit) boxes from the supermarket to hold all the odds and ends. When stacked, they will take up very little floor space.

Susan Cornelius, Hayling Island, Hampshire

Remove loose bristles from a new paintbrush, by wiping it across a piece of coarse sandpaper and then combing it out.

Madeleine Wright, Leicester

After cleaning your paintbrushes, a final rinse in water with a little fabric-softener added will leave the bristles soft and easy to use.

Mrs H M Wren, Boston, Lincolnshire

You can soften the bristles of an old paintbrush by soaking them in vinegar.

A Vincent, Edinburgh

Soak an old paintbrush in creosote before putting it away – it will keep the bristles soft.

C Townsend, London

&

Before storing a pot of paint, wrap it in clingfilm to prevent dust falling into the paint when the tin is next opened.

E Carter, Arundel, West Sussex

To prevent tools from rusting, place them in an enclosed toolbox with a few mothballs.

Robert Spencer, Aylesbury, Buckinghamshire

Plunge infrequently used tools into a small bucket of sand to prevent them from becoming rusty between each use.

Sarah Richardson, Carlisle, Cumbria

&

To remove stubborn Rawlplugs from walls, partially insert a screw. Grasp the screw with pincers and pull it out – it will withdraw the Rawlplug with it.

Julia Wheatcroft, Cambridge

If you are having difficulty removing a wood-screw, heat the end of the screwdriver.

Harry Barnes, Tunbridge Wells, Kent

To make it easier to remove a rusty screw, tighten it slightly first as this will loosen the thread.

P Carter, Arundel, West Sussex

When removing screws or small parts from a machine during repair, place them onto the adhesive side of some sticky tape in the order you remove them. It will then be easy to replace them correctly when you come to reassemble the machine.

Raymond Burger, Brickendon, Hertfordshire

If a screw pulls out of wood, stuff the hole with matchsticks and reinsert the screw.

R T Temple, Tiverton, Devon

Soap or detergent applied to the thread of a screw reduces the friction that is created as the screw enters the wood, so making insertion much easier.

K Green, London

To insert a screw into a very tight Rawlplug, first rub the thread with a wax candle.

Michael Dodds, Glasgow

To fix a screw in an odd-shaped hole, fill the hole with wet cotton wool, and then insert the screw. When dry, the cotton wool will hold the screw securely.

Antony J Harper, Weston-Super-Mare, Somerset

Wherever possible, use brass screws for securing outside fixtures because they won't corrode.

M Hooper, East Malling, Kent

To save space in your workshop, and at the same time keep your various nails and screws organised and accessible, screw the lids of old jars to the underside of a shelf. Fill the corresponding jars with the screws or nails, and then twist them back onto their lids.

Angela Stacke, London

&

To saw wood straight and smoothly, it helps to keep your index finger extended towards the tip of the saw-blade rather than clasped round the handle with the other fingers.

John H Shaw, London

When sawing wood, especially if it is damp, rub both sides of the saw-blade with a candle.

Bert Orwin, Chesterfield, Derbyshire

&

A combination of glue and sawdust makes a good wood-filler.

M Forsyth, Matlock, Derbyshire

You can use matt emulsion as a substitute for wood-primer.

Hannah Balfour, Leicester

&

To prevent hardening of left-over mastic or glue, seal the applicator tube with a lump of Blu-Tac.

M Forsyth, Matlock, Derbyshire

ॐ

If you accidentally hammer a nail into a water-pipe, tap a tapered matchstick or pencil into the hole – the wood swells and delays leakage.

D B Green, Wirral, Merseyside

If you need to drill a hole through a slippery surface, such as a tile, fix a cross made from two pieces of fabric masking tape and drill through the centre of it. The tape will enable the drill to gain a purchase.

P Carter, Arundel, West Sussex

To catch the dust when drilling a hole, tape an empty ice-cream container or light, plastic dust-pan to the wall immediately beneath the hole.

G Marshall, Rochester, Kent

When filling holes in walls, always mix the filler with the wall paint so that it matches.

C Benfield, East Malling, Kent

ॐ

To obliterate the stains made by previously damp patches on ceilings or walls, cover the area with an oil-based paint before applying emulsion.

James McMinn, Birmingham, West Midlands

To remove climbing plants from window-frames, use an old, wide-bladed wallpaper-scraper.

Susan Latimer, Midhurst, West Sussex

ॐ

When you have finished decorating a room, write on the top edge of the door the date, the design name and amount of wallpaper used, and the make and colour of paint applied. You'll be glad you did when it comes to redecorating.

Alan Price, Ferndown, Dorset

When carpeting a room, save an off-cut on which to test any cleaning products safely.

C W Edwards, Northampton

To make a small room appear larger, simply transfer the hinges to the other side of the door so that it opens against the wall.

John Ashmore, Peterborough, Cambridgeshire

When rewiring the house, have the electric sockets placed at the more convenient waist height.

Jo Elkins, London

To slide wallpaper behind a radiator without its becoming rucked, weight the bottom edge of the pasted strip with coins fastened with wooden pegs.

Karen Logan, London

࿇

When tiling, use a sink-plunger to adjust tiles; tiles will be less likely to break.

Anthea Hodson, Manningtree, Essex

Speed-clean grouting diluted bleach dispensed from an old washing-up liquid bottle. Run the nozzle along the grouting, and then rinse.

Cindy Wolfenden, Southampton, Hampshire

࿇

And a wisdom from the very boundaries of common sense ...

To save money spent on wallpaper (and educate your children at the same time), cover your children's bedroom walls with pages torn from a full-colour encyclopaedia.

D Fulford, London

Food & Drink

It's much easier to dice chicken when it's still partly frozen.

D Norman, Frodsham, Cheshire

To prevent chops from curling up, hold them under the running, cold-water tap for a minute before grilling.

Mrs E Casement, Omagh, Co Tyrone

To coat fish or chicken pieces with flour or breadcrumbs, place them in a polythene bag, tie the top, and shake the bag gently.

M J Harley, Kirkcudbright

To keep sausages moist, and to reduce their cooking time, drop them in boiling water for five minutes before cooking.

Camilla Gilbert, Kingswells, Aberdeen

ॐ

Use an old toothbrush under running water to clean celery thoroughly and effortlessly.

Mrs V Findlay-Wilson, Shaftesbury, Dorset

Soak prepared garden or organic vegetables in salted water; all the bugs and slugs will die and float to the surface.

Mrs M Snell, Ross-on-Wye, Herefordshire

Always tear lettuce-leaves by hand as knife-cut edges go brown.

Mrs J Jones, Midhurst, West Sussex

To chop up fresh herbs neatly and without waste, put them in a glass and rotate it in your hand as you chop the herbs with scissors.

Janine Kotas, Wem, Shropshire

හ

Add a bayleaf to water when cooking cabbage and similar vegetables: it eliminates the smell.

Mary Lloyd, Derby

When cooking greens, place a crust of bread in the saucepan to stop the smell.

Mrs P J Hatton, Stroud, Gloucestershire

Green vegetables will always keep their bright-green colour if a pinch of salt is added to the cooking water.

Mrs V M Wetherall, Plymouth, Devon

As a general rule, root vegetables should be placed in cold water and then brought to the boil; all others should be placed in boiling water.

Susan Webster, Derby

හ

When you roast potatoes for a special dinner, take out the centres with an apple corer and fill with rolled-up bacon rashers.

Charlotte Joseph, Lelant, Cornwall

Dunk par-boiled potatoes in a deep-fat pan before roasting. They will be evenly coated and won't need basting.

Veronica Potter, Costessey, Norfolk

To improve the flavour and texture of jacket potatoes, boil for five minutes before putting them in the oven. They'll cook quicker, too.

R H Ashby, Bristol, Somerset

New potatoes taste superlative when a little sugar is added to the cooking water.

Mrs Fay Gardiner, Seaview, Isle of Wight

To prevent potatoes turning brown in water before they are cooked, add a little milk to the water.

Mrs C Birchenough, Manchester

Pop potato waffles into a toaster until brown (about six minutes). They taste delicious, and there's no pan to clean.

Mrs M D Priestley, Sevenoaks, Kent

Add rice to your salt-shaker to stop the salt from forming lumps.

Mrs L Kettle, St Albans, Hertfordshire

To loosen any rice sticking to the bottom of the pan while cooking, stand the pan on a wet cloth for fifteen seconds.

Mrs J Green, Lancing, Sussex

Run the cold-water tap in the sink when straining pasta or vegetables: it disperses the steam.

Mrs B Andrews, Horsham, West Sussex

To give spaghetti bolognese an authentic Italian flavour, add one tablespoon of cinnamon to the sauce during cooking.

Mrs D M Coote, Oxford

෩

A milk pan will be easier to clean if you rinse it with cold water before heating the milk.

Katherine Ho, Watford, Hertfordshire

To prevent milk from boiling over, place a wooden spoon across the top of the saucepan.

Mrs Mary Furneaux, Tiverton, Devon

෩

Stewed fruit – especially apple and rhubarb – keeps its shape better if sugar is added before cooking, not during or afterwards.

Sally Major, Wadebridge, Cornwall

To remove the acidity from rhubarb, pour boiling water over it. After a few minutes, drain and cook in the usual way.

Mrs E E Busby, Reigate, Surrey

When making marmalade, don't thinly slice the Seville orange-peel; put it through a mincer.

Mrs T Cann, Biggar, Lanarkshire

ℰℬ

Make a sponge-cake lighter by adding a little soda water to the mixture.

Kate Bogle, Exeter, Devon

If, when making a cake, you find that the fat is not soft enough, try warming the sugar.

Constance Falwasser, Stockbridge, Hampshire

When taking cakes out of the oven, stand the tin on a wet dishcloth for a few minutes. The cake will then easily leave the tin.

Mrs B Heathcote, Abergavenny, Monmouthshire

Place a tea-towel over the food-mixer after adding icing sugar – it prevents clouds of sugar over the kitchen.

Mrs D Hill, Stratford-upon-Avon, Warwickshire

When transporting or storing a cake, place it on the lid of an upside-down cake-box or tin, and you will not have to struggle to take it out.

Mrs A Keates, Dartmouth, Devon

ℰℬ

To keep home-baked scones moist, wet the baking tray before cooking. The steam created prevents them from drying out.

Mrs Maureen O'Sullivan, Abingdon, Oxon

Make your biscuits and scones square instead of round to avoid having to reroll the off-cuts.

T H Hughes-Davies, Fordingbridge, Hampshire

ഔ

For lighter short pastry, use soda water instead of tap-water.

Linda Smith, Bexhill, East Sussex

For great-tasting pancakes, add the fizzy drink of your choice to the batter.

Miss Kate Burgess, Sevenoaks, Kent

To make Yorkshire puddings rise better, allow the batter to stand for at least two hours, and then beat in a desertspoonful of cold water just before cooking.

Mrs M Finch, Burton-on-Trent, Staffordshire

ഔ

To defrost sliced bread quickly, put slices in the toast-rack for a few minutes.

Sylvia Logan, Warkworth, Northumberland

When you need breadcrumbs quickly, grate a frozen loaf.

Mrs Esme Barton, Sandown, Isle of Wight

Don't waste left-over bread. Cut off the crusts and whizz in the food-processor to make crumbs. Store them in the freezer, and you have instant breadcrumbs for bread sauce, and so on.

M Lovemore, South Molton, Devon

If a piece of bread is too thick for the toaster, flatten it with a rolling-pin. (Works well with half a bagel, too.)

Graeme Alexander, Bristol, Somerset

To prevent cream-crackers and similar biscuits from breaking when you spread them with butter or cream cheese, place the cracker on a slice of bread.

Mrs S M Moss, Cranbrook, Kent

Sprinkle slices of bread with warm water before frying to stop them soaking up excess fat.

Mrs L Whittle, Oxford

For perfect fried bread, toast lightly before frying.

Mrs P A Duff, South Godstone, Surrey

છ૭

If an egg cracks as it is coming to the boil, dropping a pin into the pan will effectively seal it.

Mrs A Tiney, Bath, Somerset

When boiling eggs, place a stainless-steel tea-spoon in the saucepan: it will prevent them from cracking.

Mrs Iris Hughes, Gravesend, Kent

Poach eggs in a non-stick frying pan. They stay separate and can be easily lifted out.

Paula South, Marple, Cheshire

When whipping egg-whites, put a pinch of cream of tartar in first: they will remain stiff for longer.

Mrs P M Braddell, Exeter, Devon

After scrambling eggs in a saucepan, always wash the pan in cold water: it makes it much easier to clean it.

Mrs J Leyfield, Gloucester

If a dropped egg breaks, smother it with salt, and it will scoop up in one piece.

Mrs M Davies, Middlesborough, North Yorkshire

&

Wash and dry the top leaves of celery, and then bake in the oven until crumbly. Once cool, store in an airtight container, and use to flavour soups and stews.

Mrs E Smith, Beaconsfield, Buckinghamshire

To save time, keep a mixture of flour, salt and pepper in a shaker for flavouring meat, poultry and fish.

Mrs S Dowle, Wallasey, Merseyside

&

Mint sauce is easier to make if you add the sugar to the mint during the chopping stage.

Mrs B Ryder, Bristol, Somerset

Mix equal amounts of salad cream and tomato ketchup together to make a tasty seafood dressing.

Mrs J Gain, Chessington, Surrey

Rather than spending a lot of time making a white sauce in the traditional manner, simply put all the ingredients into a saucepan together, place over the heat, and whisk. The result is just as good.

Catherine Lacey, Devizes, Wiltshire

೫ು

Mustard will not dry in the mustard-pot if a little salt is added when mixing.

P Sherley, Leamington Spa, Warwickshire

Give mustard a more mellow flavour by mixing mustard powder with milk rather than water.

Mrs P Sargent, Bexhill, East Sussex

೫ು

To extract the kernel whole from a nut, soak in salt water overnight before cracking.

B Katz, Hove, East Sussex

To peel oranges, put them in a pan of cold water and bring to the boil. Pour off the water and peel. Result: no pith!

Mrs I M Edgington, Weybridge, Surrey

Onions peel more easily if you start removing the skin from the root end rather than from the top.

Mrs N Little, North Woodchester, Gloucestershire

80

To rescue over-salted dishes, add a few drops of milk.

P J Baker, Keyworth, Nottinghamshire

If you have added too much salt to your cooking, add a potato – it will absorb excess seasoning.

Angela Bennett, London

If you've put too much chilli in a curry, add lemon juice to reduce the effect.

Robert Austin, South Petherton, Somerset

Bitten on a green chilli? Don't try water. A teaspoon of sugar gives sure relief.

R McEvoy, London

Over-ripe tomatoes will become firm if they are placed in a basin of salted water for about twenty minutes.

Reg Davies, Reading, Berkshire

If hollandaise sauce curdles, drop in an ice-cube and continue beating until smooth.

Mrs M Yendall, Lichfield, Staffordshire

If sugar has become a solid lump, put a slice of fresh bread in with it. By the next day it will be usable.

Mrs Chloe Purton, Lampeter, Cardiganshire

Stale scones become light again after ten seconds in a microwave oven.

M Preston, Peterborough, Cambridgeshire

To restore sugary jam, add a dessertspoonful of water, stir, microwave to fast-boil, and cool. It will then be as good as freshly made.

Mrs N Halfhide, Thatcham, Berkshire

&

A glut of sweetcorn cobs will freeze perfectly for up to six months if they are still 'shrink-wrapped' in their own leaves.

Sally Major, Wadebridge, Cornwall

To keep broccoli, cauliflower, lettuce, or half-used cucumbers fresh, stand the stem (or uncut end) in a glass or bowl of water in the fridge.

Gillian Eccles, Grimsby, Lincolnshire

A double layer of kitchen roll placed in the bottom of the salad drawer in your fridge will keep all vegetables fresh for at least a week.

Mrs G H Ball, Beccles, Suffolk

Wrap the lower half of celery or leeks in kitchen paper and store in the fridge. They will keep fresh for ten days or longer.

Ellie Mac Isaac, Paisley, Renfrewshire

Grate a pound or more of peeled root-ginger and store in a covered ice-cube tray in the freezer for instant use when required.

Mrs C Taylor, Chelmsford, Essex

Do not store herbs and spices in transparent containers: light destroys their flavour.

Elizabeth Pembroke, London

Wrapping bananas in a freezer bag during hot weather prevents them from ripening too quickly and turning black.

J Rawlin, Wimborne, Dorset

Submerge unpeeled bananas in cold water for thirty minutes before use. The fruit will remain firm and won't discolour.

Alice McNally, Gravesend, Kent

To keep half a lemon fresh, place the cut side down on a small heap of sugar, and put it in the fridge.

M Wood, Whitby, North Yorkshire

ℰℭ

Keep your cheese fresh for longer by smearing a little butter on the cut edge before putting it in the fridge.

Patricia Hardie, London

Cheese will keep fresh for much longer if it is sealed in a bag with a few cardamom pods – they don't affect the flavour.

John Pilgrim, Rayleigh, Essex

To prevent cheese going damp, store it in a covered container with a lump of sugar.

Mrs T Linton, Northwood, Middlesex

ℰℭ

A clean, unpeeled potato kept in the breadbin and replaced regularly will keep your bread fresh for much longer than usual.

J Cater, Nottingham

Keep two sugar-lumps in the biscuit-tin: they will absorb any moisture and ensure that the biscuits stay crisp.

Mrs L Davie, Newbury, Berkshire

To keep cakes fresh, line your cake-tins with wax paper from breakfast-cereal packets.

Ms P Fox, Thatcham, Berkshire

Reseal packets of jumbo-sized crisps and similar dry foods by folding the top over twice and fastening with a clothes-peg.

D K Bonnett, Exeter, Devon

Pour a layer of oil over opened jars of pesto, curry paste, tomato puree, and so on. They will keep longer in the fridge.

Mrs J Buttery, Douglas, Isle of Man

Keep whistling while peeling and chopping onions, and you won't cry.

Jane Ash, Preston, Lancashire

To prevent your eyes from watering when preparing onions, place them in the freezer for ten minutes before chopping.

Elizabeth Lewis, Cardiff

ℰℴ

Cold silver foil is an excellent wine-chiller – wrap it round the bottle.

Mrs G Thompson, Stoke, Staffordshire

Fancy a quick glass of red wine at room temperature? Place your glass of wine in the microwave oven and heat on the lowest setting for one minute.

L Beilby, Stockport, Cheshire

To extract a stubborn champagne cork, twist it free with a nutcracker.

Dennis Simmonds, Hove, East Sussex

To open champagne without causing the bottle to explode, twist the bottle, not the cork.

Karen Logan, London

If you cannot finish a can of fizzy drink, put a spoon handle in the open tin and it will stay fizzy overnight.

Miss S Moelwyn-Hughes, Newmarket, Suffolk

To avoid being sprayed by the contents of a can of fizzy drink, tap sharply on the ring-pull area.

C Reeves, Wadhurst, East Sussex

Don't put fizzy drinks in the door of the fridge – the opening and shutting of the door makes them flat faster.

Mark Osborn, Sudbury, Suffolk

You will not have to remember to shake cartons of fruit juice before opening if you always store them upside down.

Mrs J M Irvin, Exeter, Devon

Freeze water in a disposable plastic cup, and use the resulting large ice-cube in your drink jugs – it will last longer than conventional-sized ice-cubes.

Steven Fessey, Gloucester

છ

You can keep tea hot for over an hour – without its becoming stewed – by removing the teabag as soon as it is brewed and covering the pot with a tea-cosy.

James Lark, Cheltenham, Gloucestershire

The netting bags supplied with dishwasher tablets are excellent for holding teabags in the pot so that you can withdraw them before the tea stews.

A E Marsden, Brighton, East Sussex

When cooking on a campfire, a green stick placed in the tea or coffee will prevent it from tasting smoky.

Mel Harris, Reedham, Norfolk

જી

For recipes requiring very specific quantities of golden syrup, use a metal spoon that you have first dipped in boiling water. The syrup will then slide off easily.

Susan Custance, Peterborough, Cambridgeshire

Use an oiled spoon to measure out honey, treacle – any sticky food that is difficult to measure precisely. It will slide off cleanly.

Mrs J Smith, York

If a recipe calls for only half an onion, use the top half. The intact root helps to preserve the lower half for future use.

Mrs L Kettle, St Albans, Hertfordshire

When you double the ingredients in a recipe, add only one and a half times as much, not twice as much, salt.

Mrs N Reynolds, Newbridge

Prior to whipping fresh cream, chill both the beater and the basin in the fridge for thirty minutes – you will get double the volume.

Mrs A O'Neill, Blaydon, Tyne & Wear

Increase the amount of juice you can extract from a lemon by microwaving it for a few seconds.

Elizabeth Douglas, Manchester

છ૭

Hold your recipe-book pages open with clothes-pegs.

Alice Coffey, Stockport, Cheshire

To remove stains from chopping boards and other food-preparation surfaces, rub them with lemon juice.

S Kingman, London

To remove any stale odour from wooden chopping boards, scrub with a weak solution of bicarbonate of soda.

Prudence Holland, London

If you use wooden chopping boards, keep one specifically for chopping onions and garlic: the wood absorbs the odour and affects other less-pungent foods that are then prepared on the same board.

Claudia Parkinson, Oxford

Lift off grease and fat from soups and stews with a piece of clingfilm.

Mandy Glancy, Prestwich, Manchester

If you can't find a plastic spoon when a recipe's directions require you to use one, clingfilm an ordinary metal one.

Mrs P Cant, Cambridge

Cover bowls and cakes with a shower-cap.

Susan Cornelius, Hayling Island, Hampshire

To silence a rattling lid on a simmering saucepan, place a short piece of string under the lid.

Mrs E B Cartmell, Chester, Cheshire

Wear latex disposable gloves when baking. No clogged fingernails; and they are easily removed if the phone rings.

Mrs M Forsyth, Stornoway, Isle of Lewis

ဆာ

And some wisdoms from the very boundaries of common sense ...

To keep your Brussel sprouts fresh and crisp, spread them out on a small area of lawn.

Mrs G Cook, Shrewsbury, Shropshire

To prevent tears when peeling onions, wear a pair of motorcycle goggles.

S Norton, London

If you do not have enough carrots for a particular dish, cut them into julienne strips.

Mrs B Haddon, Oadby, Leicestershire

To get the best flavour from a mint humbug, first eat a small piece of raw garlic.

Guy Parker, Holt, Wiltshire

If you are marooned in the Arctic, starving, remember that while you can eat polar-bear steaks with impunity, the liver is deadly poison.

Alec O'Reilly

Gardening

Feeding tomatoes with Epsom salts cures yellowing leaves.

Mrs M Huntington, Workington, Cumbria

To make sure beans, courgettes, and similar vegetables are pollinated, spray the open flowers with sweet sherry.

Mrs J Lidbrooke, Trowbridge, Wiltshire

To improve the setting of runner-beans, particularly in dry weather, plant sweet-peas in the bean row.

J R Young, Yeovil, Somerset

For big, healthy roses – and to promote a healthy root-system and prevent shock – water with a solution made from equal parts liquid soap, beer, water, and ground coffee.

Miss Manjula Passey, Birmingham, West Midlands

Throw your banana-skins on to the base of your roses. They are rich in potassium, and act as a better fertiliser than many of the ones bought from garden centres.

Audrey Routledge, Soilhull, West Midlands

Use surplus tea and used teabags to foster the growth of acid-loving plants.

Mrs D Pickthall, Barrow-in-Furness, Cumbria

ℵ

Where possible, stabilise weather-beaten daffodils by bringing two of the leaves from behind the plant and tying them in front with a reef-knot.

Mrs E J Barton, Sandown, Isle of Wight

Snapped daffodil heads will go on flowering for some time if you push the stems into the earth.

Susan Seabrook, Lower Sunbury, Middlesex

To prevent gerberas and similar flowers from drooping, push a pin into the centre of the flowerhead and down inside the stem.

Madeleine Wright, Leicester

෨

Use old teabags to cover the holes in flowerpots before adding compost for new seedlings.

W E Brown, Uxbridge, Middlesex

A redundant, pointed potato-peeler makes an excellent tool for pricking out seedlings.

J Gostelow, Retford, Nottinghamshire

Sow poppy-seed among raspberry canes. In summer, the birds will confuse the red flowers for berries and leave far more fruit.

Mrs L Bradley, East Preston, Sussex

When making up a hanging basket, wrap a small plastic bag around each plant's rootball before pushing the plant down into the compost. The bags withdraw easily when the plants are in their final places, but enable you to reposition the plant easily if necessary.

Elizabeth Cate, Denby Dale, Huddersfield

Drill holes in the bottom of plastic paint containers and use them in the greenhouse as pots for tomato plants.

Jayne Lester, Banstead, Surrey

When painted, empty 500ml tubs of luxury ice-cream make ideal flowerpots. Drill holes in the base and use the lids as saucers.

Mrs J Bickley, Daventry, Northamptonshire

For pricking out young seedlings, use old yoghurt pots and disposable plastic drinking cups: they tear open easily when planting out later on.

Mrs L Mason, Ackleton, Wolverhampton

Keep old plastic washing-up bowls as they make ideal containers for compost when potting up and transplanting seedlings.

Mrs P Moren, Faringdon, Oxfordshire

Plastic lids from large-size coffee jars make good saucers for small flowerpots.

Mrs A Penney, Southampton, Hampshire

৪১

Save disposable water-filter cartridges to provide a slow watering system for pot-plants. First soak them in water, and then push them into the soil of the container.

J G Kendall, Bristol, Somerset

Always water your garden plants using rainwater from your water-butt as it contains none of the harsh chemicals used to treat tap-water.

B A Mellor, Harrogate, Yorkshire

To make the watering of hanging baskets easier, save the cardboard tubes from toilet-tissue and push them down into the compost. They will absorb the water, drawing it down towards the roots and helping to keep the compost moist, and they will last the whole season.

Patricia Morley, Whitstable, Kent

To water delicate, newly sown seeds without disturbing them, gently squeeze water from a soaked cotton-wool ball.

R Phellas, London

To assist drainage when sewing seeds, line the seed-tray with fine grit and fill it with compost. Then sew seeds, and cover with another layer of fine grit.

Miss A Thomas, Newtown, Powys

Coffee-filter papers placed in the bottom of plant-pots will stop soil from leaking out while allowing water through.

V Simmons, Tetbury, Glouestershire

Save any polystyrene packing. Break it into pieces and use it to line the bottoms of tubs and troughs: it will retain moisture and reduce watering.

Mrs T E Holden, Carnforth, Lancashire

To prevent the nozzle of your garden hose from coming off the garden tap, rub it with soap.

A Hodson, Lawford Dale, Essex

හි

Before fixing the nozzle to your garden hose, dip the hose end into boiling water. It will soften and slip on easily.

Mrs M W Grayburn, Silverdale, Lancashire

To stop your garden hosepipe kinking on the holding reel, leave the water running whilst you wind it on.

Mrs A Ashworth, Southport, Lancashire

ॐ

A wire kitchen-trolley makes an excellent mobile greenhouse for hardening off cuttings, seedlings, and other small plants. Cover the trolley with a large polybag.

Ms Joan Carter, London

Cut two-litre plastic drink-bottles in half, and invert them over pots of cuttings or seedlings to make a mini greenhouse.

Eira Warren, Fetcham, Surrey

A lit candle left in an unheated (but lined) green-house will be enough to keep the frost off.

Rita Fitzmaurice, Heacham, Norfolk

To protect tender plants from frost and snow, cover with the clippings from coniferous plants.

Heather Owen, Chippenham, Wiltshire

To protect an outside water-tap from freezing, wrap a wet towel around it. The ice formed on the towel insulates the tap.

R A Selway, Wisbech, Cambridgeshire

Use chicken-feed to melt ice on paths: it doesn't damage plants like salt, and the birds will eat it once the ice has gone.

Rajiv Bobal, Poole, Dorset

 formula

To keep flies away from your organic carrots, sprinkle used coffee grindings along the rows throughout the growing season.

E L Campbell, Bexhill, East Sussex

To keep caterpillars off cabbages and cauliflower, steep some rhubarb leaves in boiling water and leave until the water has cooled. Then remove the leaves, and pour the water over the plants.

Mrs K Hoole, Market Drayton, Shropshire

Bran, baked and crushed eggshells, or holly leaves sprinkled around the bases of plants are very effective slug and snail deterrants while being safe for pets and birds.

Paul Vines, Horley, Surrey

103

Place fir-cones on the soil surface of pots containing shrubs: they reduce evaporation, discourage slugs, and look attractive too.

Mrs W E Fuller, Machynlleth, Powys

To remove dead slugs from the garden without damaging your plants, use a pair of old food-tongs.

K Denby, Bradford, West Yorkshire

Make a trap for earwigs: turn a flowerpot upside down and put hay underneath it. By the next day you will find the pot will have attracted a number of these pests.

D Fulford, London

Pour the soapy water from the washing-up or laundry over your rose-bushes to keep them greenfly free.

K M McCarthy, Llanelly, Carmarthen

When potting up, put a dusting of ant-powder into the bottom of plantpots to deter ants from taking up residence.

F Barker, Cambridge

To eradicate moles from your lawn, scoop small trowel-loads of used cat-litter into and under the mounds.

Vivienne S Tennant, St Keverne, Cornwall

To halt the progress of moles across your lawn, place half a raw onion face down on each hill.

L Weber, Huntingdon, Cambridgeshire

If children want to keep a dead stag-beetle cara-
pace, place it near an ants' nest and the ants will
clean the inside.

Lorraine Hepburn, Fetcham, Surrey

ॐ

If your pressure-sprayer does not have wheels,
you can make it mobile by attaching it to a garden trolley with an elastic luggage-strap.

J Jones, Sutton Coldfield, West Midlands

Secure old pop-socks to the end of a guttering
pipe to prevent debris from entering your water-
butt.

Charlotte Primrose, Newcastle upon Tyne

Knock through the top and bottom of a cardboard box to make a frame for the inside of a garden rubbish-bag.

A Hodson, Lawford Dale, Essex

Keep an old saucepan in your compost-bag to
lift the compost out easily.

Miss Pat Goodey, Worthing, West Sussex

ॐ

To keep terracotta pots looking new, treat the
outside with any water-seal preservative.

Roger Hayes, Swindon, Wiltshire

Save leftover suds from 'wash n wax' car cleaning as they are excellent for washing muddy garden tools and kids' bikes without causing them
to rust. They also make wellies shine again.

Peter Hitchings, Crediton, Devon

Soak rusty garden tools in a bucket of wallpaper-paste for a few hours, and they'll come up like new.

Mrs Hetty Fletcher, Budleigh Salterton, Devon

Cut holes in the toes of an old pair of mules, and nail them up in the garden shed. They make excellent mounted holders for secateurs and shears.

Jill Wright, Tavistock, Devon

To save time spent searching for your shears or scissors while working in the garden, put the points in the ground when you are not using them.

Mrs J Simkins, Welford, Northamptonshire

Utilise a broken garden fork or blunt spade by sticking it in the ground by the door and using it as a boot-scraper.

Jack Leaman, Leicester

For simpler gardening, try using a paint-scraper –
it replaces trowel, hand- fork, hoe, and chopper.

Mrs S G Butcher, Newcastle, Staffordshire

ʿ⃝

Use the spare cuts of rubber carpet-underlay as
kneelers in the garden.

Mrs D Pover, Brighton, East Sussex

Before throwing out old dining-room chairs,
press out the padded seat-panels for use as kneelers
in the garden.

D K Bonnett, Exeter, Devon

The leather gloves that you can buy very cheaply
from charity shops are excellent for gardening:
they fit better than cotton gloves, and are a lot
stronger.

Mrs N H Strathern, Torrington, Devon

ʿ⃝

Create a bird-bath by removing the handles from
saucepans or frying pans and placing a stone in the
centre for the birds to land on.

Ann Marshall, Glasgow

A decorator's paint-tray makes a good, inexpensive bird-bath – the small birds love the shallow
end; the large ones the deep.

John Gibbens, Norwich, Norfolk

ʿ⃝

Use a vegetable-strainer to skim unwanted duck-
weed from your pond.

Anon

To clear a pond of blanket-weed, twirl a sturdy, rough twig in the water, and wind out the weed stuck to it.

Mrs M Pickles, Clitheroe, Lancashire

જી

To remove dandelions permanently, cut off the foliage to expose the root-tops, and smother these with salt.

V Warner, Tetford, Shropshire

Goose-grass and thistles are easier to pull up if you wait until they have started to flower.

P Kirk, Bradford, Yorkshire

Seven layers of newspaper under two to three inches of soil make a very effective and invisible weed-barrier that lasts for years.

Linda Davis, London

Use empty kitchen- or bathroom-cleaner spray containers for spraying weedkiller onto plants. They can then be disposed of without washing out.

D L Carter, West Grinstead, West Sussex

જી

When erecting canes for runner-beans, cross them halfway up rather than near the top: this way, the beans will hang outside the cane support, so making them easier to pick.

Mrs I G Martin, Margate, Kent

Bind the cane supporting your runner-beans with the plastic ties used by electricians. The ties will not loosen or break, however strong the wind.

Ted Jones, Cardiff

To prevent bamboo canes from splitting, place a spent gun-cartridge over the end of the cane before hammering it into the ground.

Mrs J Price, Maldon, Essex

Before using new bamboo canes, wind fine, plastic-coated wire around each end, and secure with a knot. This will help to stop them splitting, and so make them last longer.

Mrs J Price, Maldon, Essex

༁

Plant bindweed roots with plants that require tying to stakes – it will save time and string as they grow together.

A A Faucheux, Henley-on-Thames, Oxon

Plastic cable-clips nailed onto walls make excellent tie-points to support climbing plants and roses.

Colin Brooks, Northleach, Gloucestershire

To prevent border-plants tumbling over wet paths, tie them back with dental-floss rather than garden twine. It is invisible, strong, and very long lasting.

K M Egleston, Basingstoke, Hampshire

༁

For the first lawn-cut of the season, use an old blade in the mower so that any stones that may be hidden in the grass from the winter don't ruin a new blade.

D Lloyd, Wirral, Merseyside

Warm the engine of your petrol lawnmower for five minutes with an old hairdryer. It will start first time.

John Rudkin, Little Eversden, Cambridgeshire

To make it easier to remove grass-cuttings from the blades of your hover-mower, apply car polish to the underside before you cut the lawn.

V Warner, Tetford, Shropshire

To remove fairy-rings from lawns, insert a garden fork as deeply as possible into them, and then squirt neat detergent into the holes.

P Roberts, Sandiacre, Nottinghamshire

To clear moss easily from the lawn, move hens in a wire-run to the affected area. They'll scratch out the moss, and – as a bonus – keep you supplied with eggs.

Mrs H Robinson, Lower Tysoe, Warwickshire

When edging a lawn after mowing, alternate the direction in which you proceed each time and you will achieve a much cleaner edge.

C F Baum, Hinckley, Leicestershire

When putting wooden garden furniture out, place the legs in empty tin-cans to help prevent them from rotting.

C G Welborn, Petersfield, Hampshire

When erecting a wooden fence, prevent the feet from rotting by wrapping plastic around them before sinking them into the ground.

Miss P M Alexander, Stonehaven, Grampian

෨

When clipping the hedge, lay a polythene bag on the ground to catch the trimmings – it will save a lot of time spent in clearing up.

G Hardwick, Dronfield, Derbyshire

To prevent mint from spreading beyond its designated boundary, plant a few sprigs in a medium-size plantpot and bury it in the ground.

N M Walsh, Warrington, Cheshire

To avoid sun-dazzle while watching pondlife, site a new garden pond to the north.

J Winchester, Barnstaple, Devon

To attract birds to your bird-bath, place brightly coloured marbles in the water.

Rosanne Haselden, Sevenoaks, Kent

When you've broken a shrub with your football, you can disguise the break by rubbing it with damp soil.

R Moore, Kenilworth, Warwickshire

෨

If you have a mole colony in your garden, make the best of it by collecting the soil from the hills – it makes great top-dressing for lawns or for potting on plants.

Mrs M J Osman, Guildford, Surrey

And some wisdoms from the very boundaries of common sense ...

Pile a few leaves in small heaps around the garden: every morning chop up the attracted slugs and leave them in place: this attracts more to destroy the following morning!

J Young, Bristol, Somerset

To distinguish an adder from a harmless grass-snake, look closely into its eyes: the adder's pupils are slits, the grass-snake's round.

John Hayward

Health & Beauty

If a stiff leg makes climbing stairs difficult, sling a tie behind the affected knee. Holding the ends of the tie, lift the leg up each step.

Veronica Hall, Leeds, Yorkshire

To flush away stiffness in joints or muscles, drink small cupfuls of boiled water throughout the day from a prepared thermos-flask.

Joy Ricketts, Honiton, Devon

For relief from pain in the neck or shoulders, try resting against a small beanbag (available from pet shops).

Mrs J Coker, Kenilworth, Warwickshire

If you suffer from a bad back, invest in some silk pyjamas and sheets to make sliding out of bed in the morning easy.

Sarah Price, Bristol, Somerset

For those with bad backs and difficulty bending, a four-foot-long garden cane with Blu-Tac attached is wonderful for picking up your post.

Miss T Bennett, Buckhurst Hill, Essex

If you have difficulty bending to put on shoes or tie up shoelaces, put your foot on the second or third stair.

P Jackson, Cockermouth, Cumbria

Dab some ordinary salt on the end of your tongue when suffering from cramp. Instant relief!

Mrs S Bent, Nottingham

ℰℭ

Polish fingernails with an old electric toothbrush.

Judith Rydings, Great Missenden, Buckinghamshire

To dry nail varnish quickly, plunge wet nails into ice-cold water.

Mrs G Thompson, Stoke, Staffordshire

To strengthen flaky nails quickly, paint them daily with tea-tree oil.

Mrs S Knight, Esher, Surrey

To make your nails look longer for that special occasion, paint the top third of your nail with nail-tip whitener.

H Chotoye, Gloucester

A one-a-day evening-primrose-oil capsule will greatly improve the quality and strength of fingernails.

M E Ashmore, Douglas, Isle of Man

Trim your fingernails just before you go to bed, and the natural overnight growth will smooth over ragged edges.

James Slater, Dudley, Tyne & Wear

Always cut fingernails and toenails after a bath when they're much softer.

D Howard, Banstead, Surrey

Cut toenails in the bath under water. The clippings won't fly everywhere.

M Standing, Chandlers Ford, Hampshire

The bitter, milky sap of dandelion stalks rubbed onto fingernails will deter nail-biting.

Ben Heap, Sheffield, Yorkshire

∞

If, after gardening, you are finding it difficult to shift ingrained dirt from your hands, wash your hair. The hair will act as a gentle scourer. It works wonders!

Carole Cronin, Chelmsford, Essex

A mixture of lard and sugar will cleanse hands of stains and dirt.

K Crookhall, Stamford, Lincolnshire

To smooth and soften rough hands, mix a teaspoon of sugar and baby-oil together, and rub into the hands. Rinse in warm water.

Mrs J Buttery, Douglas, Isle of Man

To whiten hands quickly, just smooth on a little lemon juice.

S Webster, London

Fade age-spots on the hands quickly by rubbing castor oil into them for a few nights.

E Spencer, Aylesbury, Buckinghamshire

To prevent that shivery feeling after swimming, dry your hands and wrists first.

Mrs A Heath, Poynton, Cheshire

If you have arthritic hands, smother them with vegetable oil before putting on rubber gloves and washing up in hot water.

Susan Latimer, Midhurst, West Sussex

ହେ

To relieve cold or tired feet, cut and insert an inlay of bubble-wrap in your shoes. Use several layers for wellies.

Mrs E Hamilton, Bristol, Somerset

If your wellies leak, wrap your feet in freezer bags before putting the wellies on.

Catherine Lacey, Devizes, Wiltshire

Sprinkle talcum powder into shoes to prevent bare feet getting hot and sticky.

Mrs R Linton, Dorking, Surrey

Banish the most stubborn verucca by rubbing it daily with a banana-skin.

V Warner, Tetford, Shropshire

To relieve the discomfort of chillblains, rub the affected part with a piece of celery.

Mrs J Wood, London

To prevent soft corns, use a tissue to dry thoroughly between the toes after bathing.

S Murray, Whitstable, Kent

Use dry-skin lotion on your feet as well as your hands and body. It will keep your feet supple, and discourage the growth of hard skin.

J E Willdig, Solihull, West Midlands

ॐ

If you have a cold bathroom, or have run too much cold water into your bath, use bubble-bath. The bubbles help to retain whatever heat there is in the water.

Helen Hirst, Huddersfield, West Yorkshire

Make shampoo-time for children more fun and less painful – let them wear swimming goggles or a snorkelling mask.

Mrs J Tilbury, Weybridge, Surrey

Save on shampoo by working from the back of your head to the front. Much less is used.

J Burns, Chard, Somerset

If your hair is suffering from the effects of hard water, add one tablespoon of bicarbonate of soda to the washing and rinsing water.

R & I Harding, Frinton-on-Sea, Essex

To treat cradle-cap, use the prescribed shampoo, then comb through with a steel nit-comb. The dead skin will fall out in one treatment.

J Morris, Doncaster, South Yorkshire

ॐ

When washing or dressing in a steamy bathroom, prevent your from frizzing or drooping by wearing a shower-cap.

Miss J Roche, Rayleigh, Essex

Run the adhesive side of sticky tape over the inside of your collar after visiting the hairdresser to get rid of any irritating, loose bits of hair.

Mrs L Henderson, Reading, Berkshire

When brushing your hairstyle into place, don't be tempted to snip off any awkward strands, just use a warm hairdryer to put them back into place.

Paula Hagerty, Peterborough, Cambridgeshire

When you've run out of hairspray, a wire coat-hanger brushed over your head will rid your hair of static.

Carol Hunt, Newcastle upon Tyne

ॐ

To help slow hair-loss, rub the affected area with half a raw onion until the skin is red and tingling.

Jonathan Jarvis, Chesterfield, Derbyshire

ॐ

Gentlemen, after conditioning your hair in the shower, rub the lather onto your beard, then wet-shave. You will get a much closer shave than usual.

Martin W Robinson, London

If you use a foil-type electric razor, turn the cutter round 180 degrees from time to time. You will get a better shave.

G Watson, Chippenham, Wiltshire

When shaving with shaving foam, a few drops of shampoo in the rinse water will dissolve the foam and let the whiskers sink.

Robin C Potts, Uxbridge, Middlesex

If an aerosol shaving cream is running low, stand it in hot water each day before use. It will last about two more weeks.

R S Rossant, Manchester

☙

To make a roll of cotton wool last twice as long as usual, unravel the roll, and either drape it over a hot radiator or place it in an airing cupboard – it will double in size.

Carol Small, Clevedon, Somerset

Soap will last longer if you store it in the airing cupboard for a few weeks before use.

Miss H Johnson, Seaford, East Sussex

To use up ends of soap, cut a slit in a sponge and place soap pieces into it. This creates a delightfully soapy bath sponge.

Sheila Smith, Coulsdon, Surrey

If you have a shampoo bottle with a screw-on cap, drill a hole in the top to make a handy dispenser and save yourself endless searches for the lid.

Mrs Freda Roles, Oadby, Leicestershire

&

If you have worn your lipstick down to the casingp, pop it into the freezer. When frozen, carefully lift out the stub. Press some softened candle wax into the empty casing and then replace the lipstick stub.

Mrs P H Wolfe, London

By taking three lipstick colours on holiday, you can achieve seven different colour combinations to suit your entire holiday wardrobe.

Cheryl McKeracher, Farnham, Surrey

Use up ends of lipsticks with a lip-brush for many more weeks of use.

A James, Carshalton, Surrey

Place your eye- or lip-liner pencils in the freezer for fifteen minutes before sharpening. You will find it easier to sharpen them and to produce a fine point.

Carolyn Choong, New Malden, Surrey

&

Leave a skewer in your make-up bottles to dispense the desired amount of cream without unnecessary wastage.

Emma Williams, Wrexham, Clwyd

When your thick plastic tube of cosmetic seems empty, cut it in half and scoop out the remaining contents. The amount will surprise you.

Winifred Peden, Esher, Surrey

To prevent lids sticking on nail varnish, lip fixatives, etc., smear the neck of the bottles with petroleum jelly or moisturiser.

Mrs J C Gingell, Bury St Edmonds, Suffolk

In cold, frosty weather, keep your make-up remover and face-creams in the airing cupboard.

Mrs V Findlay-Wilson, Shaftesbury, Dorset

When applying mascara, keep your mouth open and you won't stick the brush in your eyes.

Carolyn Hallinger, Andover, Hampshire

If you wear spectacles, and can't see to apply eye make-up, break an old pair across the bridge and wear one half at a time.

Mrs Morag Stobbart, Corbridge, Northumberland

When plucking eyebrows, a little babies' teething gel applied to the area will make the process less painful.

Judith Rydings, Great Missenden, Buckinghamshire

Use a decorator's radiator paint-roller to apply fake tan to areas such as your back.

Mrs B Naylor, Farnborough, Hampshire

To make a dark foundation lighter, mix the required amount in the palm of your hand with a drop or two of moisturiser.

I Walsh, Wigan, Manchester

જી

If you have difficulty inserting earrings into pierced ears, simply moisten the ear-lobes: they will slip in easily.

Mrs P Ashley, Maidstone, Kent

Never spray perfume or lacquer when wearing real or fake pearls. It will discolour them.

Mrs D M Coote, Oxford

જી

If you are allergic to metal alloys, coat the back of metal objects with a thick layer of nail polish.

Angela Joslin, Ipswich, Suffolk

To stop itching, and soothe an allergic skin reaction or heat-rash, rub the affected area with the inside of a banana skin.

Mrs J Avery, Weymouth, Dorset

To sooth itchy skin, rub it with the inside of a banana-skin.

Charles Cleall, Ashford, Middlesex

To cure nappy-rash, heat some olive oil, add one teaspoon of dried camomile flowers, and leave to infuse. When cool, strain the oil and then smooth it over the rash. It will clear up in two days.

Mrs P Child, Norwich, Norfolk

Never hang 'next to skin' washing out in frosty weather as it can cause skin irritation. This particularly applies to nappies.

Veronica Taylor, Milton Keynes, Buckinghamshire

ଚ

To keep your head cool in summer, place a cabbage- or lettuce-leaf in your hat.

Ms E Patricia Kingswell, Camberley, Surrey

Bio-yoghurt is a marvellous soother for sunburn.

Mrs M Barnett, Braunton, North Devon

To take the heat out of sunburn, cut a tomato in two and apply to the affected area.

N Lucas, Daventry, Northamptonshire

ଚ

A dab of toothpaste is a good emergency soother for mosquito-bites.

Mrs A Sawyer, Stamford, Lincolnshire

To relieve the itching caused by a mosquito-bite, apply a hot wrung-out flannel to the area.

Gillian Eccles, Grimsby, Lincolnshire

The freshly cut surface of an onion will provide relief from stings.

R Harding, Huntingdon, Cambridgeshire

Wasp-sting? Rub the area with damp soap frequently for the first hour, and then occasionally for the next two to three hours. The pain will soon go.

Miss B A Moore, Leigh On Sea, Essex

When stung by nettles, rub the skin with garden mint – its more effective than a dock-leaf .

Mrs J Worthington, Stanstead, Essex

෨

Garlicky breath can be cured by chewing the non-printed edges of a newspaper.

Mrs D Haines, Cambridge

Before taking unpleasant medicine, suck an ice-cube to numb your tastebuds.

Miss G F Rae, Balfron Station, Glasgow

A few days before visiting the dentist, practise keeping your mouth open for a few minutes – it will help to prevent your jaw aching while in the chair.

Mrs E Avery, Maidstone, Kent

Put a baby's spoon or teaspoon in the fridge or freezer: once cold it will relieve teething problems effectively and cheaply.

Mrs J Roberts, Alton, Hampshire

When cleaning dentures, place a flannel in the basin so that if they should slip out of your hands they won't break.

Mrs D Kazana, Nottingham

If you have toothache, suck on a clove until you see your dentist. The comforting warmth from the clove eases the pain.

Mrs S Mullinger, Boscombe, Dorset

Avoid lacerating your tongue on a broken tooth by chewing gum. This keeps your tongue away from tooth until you can visit the dentist.

V A Harrison, Solihull, West Midlands

To avoid the frustration of having to squeeze the tube repeatedly to extract toothpaste, keep the tube standing upside down.

Angela Bennet, London

For emergency treatment of mouth-ulcers and sore gums, rub desensitising toothpaste onto the affected area.

Amanda Warwick, Saffron Walden, Essex

To stop a cold-sore developing, dab on aftershave or neat perfume immediately you get the tingling feeling.

G Heath, Welwyn Garden City, Hertfordshire

To stop bleeding in the mouth, suck a spoonful of brown sugar.

S Murray, Whitstable, Kent

ઈઝ

To ensure a peaceful night when you are suffering from a cough, place a saucer containing a piece of brown paper soaked in vinegar by the bed.

Geoff B Hamer, Wantage, Oxon

Holding both arms up as high as possible over your head will stop even the severest coughing fit within a matter of seconds.

E Knight, London

A spoonful of honey a day keeps hay-fever at bay.

Hannah Atkins, Matlock, Derbyshire

ઈઝ

To remove half a splinter, cover the area with a small square of damp bread and a plaster, and leave overnight.

Mrs Clare Drewett, Bournemouth, Dorset

To remove a difficult splinter, mix a little soap and sugar, apply it to the area and cover with a plaster. Leave for twenty-four hours.

Mrs W H Thomas, Droitwich, Worcestershire

ℬ

To cure hiccups, suck a slice of lemon and swallow the juice – instant remedy!

J C Reed, Great Missenden, Buckinghamshire

Stop hiccups immediately with a teaspoonful of malt vinegar.

John H Shaw, London

ℬ

If a ring is tight and difficult to remove, hold your hand over your head while you remove it.

Muriel Brocklehurst, Stalybridge, Cheshire

If you bruise your arm, slide a wine-chiller onto it to reduce the swelling. It's more efficient than frozen peas.

Ruth and Alice Burkitt, Ashwell, Hertfordshire

ℬ

Lettuce is a good cure for insomnia if it is eaten immediately before retiring.

Mrs R Linton, Dorking, Surrey

Can't get to sleep? Decide very firmly that you will stay awake all night, and see what happens.

Miss D Davidson, Teignmouth, Devon

Soothe away a hard day's stress by dropping a peppermint teabag into the bath for a pick-me-up.

R A Smith, London

If you are too tired to sleep, put your feet under running cold water for a few minutes.

Karen Logan, London

&

When you are dazzled by low sun, a tennis-visor is much more effective than sunglasses.

Mrs A R Anderson, Bridport, Dorset

Use talcum powder to remove sand sticking to bodies – wet or dry.

Tim La Haye, New Malden, Surrey

&

To save a doctor's time on call-outs, have your medical history and details of current medication to hand on a notepad.

L F Shapton, Plasmarl, Swansea

When requiring an emergency bandage to secure a dressing, use a strip of clingfilm. It will remain firmly in place for several hours.

Jane Dunning, Romsey, Hampshire

ဆာ

And some wisdoms from the very boundaries of common sense ...

Squeeze toothpaste on to finger, rub on to teeth, distribute with tongue. This saves toothpaste being left in the brush's bristles

Mrs Mary Mathias, Penrith, Cumbria

To relieve cramp, grasp both ear-lobes between thumbs and first fingers and waggle furiously. Seems ridiculous, but it works!

Mrs Miller, Warrington, Cheshire

To unblock your nose, place a tennis ball under your arm and squeeze against your body lightly for one minute.

Simon Cole, London

To get rid of a wart, rub it with raw meat, bury the meat, and as the meat rots the wart will disappear.

H T Richards, Telford, Shropshire

Indoor Plants & Flowers

To remove greenfly swarms from roses inside the house or in wedding decorations, blow with a cool hairdryer.

T. Walken, Southport, Merseyside

જી

To protect cut flowers and plants when transporting them, put them into a cut-down two-litre plastic bottle.

V Warner, Tetford, Shropshire

Want a tub to fit your pot plant or vice versa? Measure the diameter and depth of the pot or plant, and then make a cut-out of it. Take the cut-out with you when you go to the garden centre.

Mrs M Webster, Leicester

જી

If your favourite vase is leaking, coat the inside with hot wax and leave it to harden. Once dry, it will provide a protective, waterproof film that will enable you to use the vase again.

Mrs M A Firth, Pontefract, West Yorkshire

A cracked vase can be brought back into use if it is carefully lined with foil to make it watertight.

Mrs P A Gregory, Cheltenham, Gloucestershire

જી

To keep houseplants watered while you are away on holiday, place a well-soaked piece of foam in a washing-up bowl, cover it with water, and place your pot-plants on top.

Mrs A I Thompson, Southsea, Hampshire

To keep the leaves of rubber-plants clean and shiny, wipe with a solution made from half-milk, half-water, and a few drops of vegetable oil.

Isobel Moules, Virginia Water, Surrey

Wet-wipes are excellent for removing dust and cobwebs from the leaves of indoor decorative foliage plants.

L B Bloom, Salisbury, Wiltshire

&

You can revive a drooping pot-plant by wrapping it whole in damp newspaper, and then storing it in a dark place for twenty-four hours.

Stella Hall, Pewsey, Wiltshire

Drooping cut roses will perk up if you cut the stems and plunge them into boiling water for a few minutes.

V Warner, Tetford, Shropshire

Spray-carnations will last much longer than usual if you remove any buds before arranging them i your vase.

Celia Sharman, London

Make foxglove-tea to lengthen the life of cut-flowers: steep a handful of leaves in boiling water; next day, strain, and add to the vase-water.

Sally Moore, London

When arranging tulips in a vase, make a pin-hole at the base of the flower, where it joins the stalk, to stop them flopping.

P Butt, Sutton Coldfield, West Midlands

If the stems of cut flowers are very short and difficult to arrange, insert the stems into waxed drinking-straws.

Mrs D Clements, Ballymena, Co Antrim

To give your flower arrangements a professional look, fill your vase with water, and then place clingfilm tightly over the top. Pierce this with the stems.

Mrs K Manley, Loughton, Essex

Buy flowers from a flower stall – the stallholders have little storage space so their blooms are usually fresher.

Gill Merritt, London

If you buy flowers in bud, stand them in a vase of lemonade to bring them into flower and make them last longer.

Angela Moules, Salisbury, Wiltshire

Out & About

If you aren't travelling by car, use a basket in the supermarket – never buy more than you can carry.

Mrs D K Smith, Chester, Cheshire

At the supermarket, pack your groceries according to which cupboard they are stored in to save time when unpacking at home.

S Overell, Tarrington, Devon

❧

When planning an unfamiliar car journey, allow at least half an hour more than ought to be necessary: you'll use up the time in getting lost and arguing with your spouse.

P Kirk, Bradford, Yorkshire

When going somewhere by bus, get fit and save some money by getting off at the stop before your final destination and walking the rest of the way.

Mrs K Brock, Aylesbury, Buckinghamshire

When walking up a long or steep hill, look down at your feet. It will make the walk much easier.

F Green, Grantham, Lincolnshire

If you need to walk or cycle on unlit roads, attach a few CDs – shiny side out – to your back as reflectors.

K Fricker, Buckfastleigh, Devon

❧

When learning to swim, find a pool filled with sea-water – it makes you more buoyant.

Mrs Marion Newman, Leicester

When going swimming, put your towel in the locker last – no need to wet your clothes with damp hands to find it.

Michael Gilligan, Bolton, Lancashire

❧

When travelling light, put pills, powders and potions in camera-film cases, and label them accordingly.

P Riley, Beccles, Suffolk

Share clothes between suitcases when packing for a holiday. If one case is lost, you will have enough essentials to prevent a spoilt holiday.

M A Walsh, Glossop, Derbyshire

When packing for a holiday, roll your clothes, rather than laying them flat: they take up less space this way.

Mary E Barnett, Braunton, Devon

When packing a suitcase, keep pleated skirts in place with a strip of sticky tape around the hem.

Ms M Anderson, Bournemouth, Dorset

When packing for a holiday, fold clothes neatly and then place them in individual plastic bags. Anything you need will then slip out easily without disturbing the whole case.

Mrs A Keates, Dartmouth, Devon

To remove creases from your clothes while you are on holiday, blow hot air from your hairdryer on to them.

Mrs Dora Doyle, Ormskirk, Lancashire

ഔ

Take your vegetable knife and tin-opener on self-catering holidays. The ones provided are usually a struggle to use.

Mrs J Cowdrill, Sutton Coldfield, West Midlands

Freeze milk before taking it on a camping holiday: it will keep fresh for longer, and it will also act as an ice-pack for other packed foods.

Mrs S Shepherd, East Dean, East Sussex

Take a roll of sticky tape with you on holiday to reseal tubes of suntan lotion, etc. before repacking for your journey home.

H J Carlo, Colchester, Essex

Take a large lump of Blu-Tac on holiday. It comes in very useful as an emergency plug.

Amanda Warwick, Saffron Walden, Essex

A portable kitchen-timer is an ideal, easy-to-set alarm to take on holidays with you, and it doesn't take up much space in your bag..

J Rippon, London

Always pack some bubble-wrap in your suitcase when you go on holiday: it comes in very handy for packing fragile souvenirs and duty-free bottles!

Miss A Cottier, Tamworth, Staffordshire

Use the waterproof cover designed for a rotary-airer to ensure your beach umbrella survives the flight and luggage carousel. It fits perfectly!

Ms H Brierley, Leicester

හ

To settle a wobbly four-legged table in a restaurant, place a small piece of bread under the offending leg. It awill djust itself automatically to suit.

David Sinclair, Malaga, Spain

When visiting a pantomime or theatre, take a carrier-bag in which to put your coat before placing it under the seat.

Norma J Mallory, Brentwood, Essex

When attending morning service in a church in winter, don't forget your hot-water bottle!

Caroline Buddery, Great Yarmouth, Norfolk

හ

If, while you are out on your bicycle, one of the tyres is badly punctured, stuff the tyre with grass. It will at least get you home.

Ray James, Eastbourne, Sussex

During icy-weather spells, place a magnet on your car's lock every evening. It will prevent it from freezing up.

Mrs Prudence Holland, London

To remove tar or black oil from feet or shoes after walking on a beach, dab with material or cotton wool dipped in suntan oil.

Mrs P Richards, London

137

When on holiday, remove beach-tar from your shoes and skin by using suntan cream or butter. Rub well, using a tissue, and rinse off.

R Lawler, Burwell, Cambridgeshire

છ

When travelling by plane, attach a distinctively coloured ribbon to the handle of your suitcase for ease of recognition at baggage reclaim.

John McQuade, France

In case your credit-cards are stolen or lost, stick the card-cancellation phone number on a label on the underside of your shoe instep.

Mrs Josephine Lane, Uppingham, Rutland

To protect your wallet from pick-pockets, wrap two broad elastic bands around it. This makes it very difficult to pull from you pocket.

B J Hall, Polstead, Suffolk

If you are travelling to an area where you are at risk of being mugged, fill a spare wallet with out-of-date credit-cards to give up to thieves.

John Lawrence, London

Note the names and numbers displayed on trades-men's vans parked by schools, hospitals, or other public buildings – government departments don't employ cowboys.

T L Jones, Cardiff

Tie a length of bright ribbon to your car-keys: they will be easier to find when they have worked their way to the bottom of your handbag.

Midge Wise, Holford, Somerset

Drivers: avoid forgetting to take something vital with you by placing the item with your car-keys – you can't leave without it.

M Seller, Bracknell, Berkshire

&

While you are away on holiday, leave old shoes outside the door. Get someone to rearrange them on a daily basis to give the impression that the house is occupied.

Mrs B Watts, King's Lynn, Norfolk

To catch mail while you are away on holiday, suspend a cardboard box from two hooks attached to the inside of the door under the letterbox. It will save you from having to force the door open on your return.

Mrs T D Crossland, Bedford

Before you go on holiday, place half a lemon in every room. The house will smell fresh and welcoming when you return.

F I Cramp, Cromer, Norfolk

Before going on holiday, write the names and addresses of all likely recipients of holiday post-cards in a small notebook, and take that with you rather than risk losing your address book..

Mrs B Cox, Sudbury, Suffolk

છે

Keep a dustbin bag in the car. When you come back with a wet umbrella, pop it in the bag to keep the car dry.

Dorothy Woods, Bolton, Lancashire

Keep an old raincoat in the boot of the car. It is handy for breakdowns and unexpected showers.

G Wagstaff, Southend-on-Sea, Essex

Keep a coolbox in the boot of your car for cold and frozen food-shopping.

M H Surridge, Windsor, Berkshire

When you renew your telephone address book, keep the old one in your car: it will come in very useful for those occasions when you need to con-tact friends or family when you are away from home.

Mrs D Page, Bishops Stortford, Hertfordshire

Protect a hat or a plant while travelling by placing it in an inflated plastic bag.

Anthea Hodson, Manningtree, Essex

છે

To prevent slipping in frosty weather, dab the heels of your boots or shoes with methylated spirit.

Mrs P J Hatton, Stroud, Gloucestershire

To prevent slipping on icy pavements, put a wide strip of fabric-plaster across the tread of each shoe-sole.

Ms N McDonald, Lincoln, Lancashire

To improve road-holding on icy days, carry a heavy weight (such as a sack of potatoes) in the car boot.

P Jackson, Cockermouth, Cumbria

&

Thread two elastic bands over your handbag handle to stop it slipping off your shoulder.

Mrs L Boardman, Hereford

When carrying rucksacks, carry each other's – you can then remove the item you want easily because another person's back is easier to get at than your own.

Mrs J E Wolfe, Halifax, Yorkshire

&

To ease parking in a small garage, suspend a light, brightly coloured beachball where the windscreen centre should come to rest (or the rear window, if reversing in).

P K Lewis, Hyde, Cheshire

Do you have difficulty getting out of a car? Place two plastic bags on the seat and swivel round.

Mrs K Gibbard, Slough, Berkshire

It is easier to get out of the back seat of a two-door car backwards than forwards.

Mrs L M Morgan, Penllwyn Park, Camarthen

142

ॐ

Pack your family's toothbrushes for a holiday in a rubber glove – one brush per finger.

M Saarto, Guildford, Surrey

To counter the effects of unsafe water when travelling in tropical climes, brush your teeth night and morning with a teaspoon of whisky.

Mrs Maureen Thurston, Hertford

ॐ

Don't keep bank or credit-cards near the magnetic clasp on a wallet or handbag – they can affect the cards' magnetic strips, and invalidate them.

Vera Naylor, Scarborough, Yorkshire

Keep a plastic camera-film container full of coins in the car: ready cash for car parking, phone calls, shopping trolleys, and so on.

W Parkes, Wollaton, Nottingham

Keep one of the empty metal tubes in which large cigars are purchased, and use it to store £1 coins for parking meters.

Elizabeth Shaw, London

ॐ

Take a magnet with you when you go to buy any stainless-steel item, such as a saucepan, to ensure you are not charged top price for low-grade steel – high-grade stainless steel is non-magnetic.

Richard E Hill, Tunbridge Wells, Kent

ॐ

And some wisdoms from the very boundaries of common sense ...

Time your baby's nappy change to coincide with your visit to the supermarket and take advantage of the nappies in the baby changing room.
    Mrs A Oliphant, Milton Keynes, Buckinghamshire

Use the free postcards provided at major cinemas to contact a friend.
        Stephen Fessey, Birmingham, West Midlands

When washing your hands away from home, hold rings in your mouth so you don't leave them behind.
        Sarah Mayhead, Drumagg Barracks

Do not join a queue until it is reduced to four people.
            Ms M Irwin, Belfast

If you do not have a 10-franc piece for your hypermarket trolley in France, a Polish zloty will work.
    Peter J Cullis, Chalfont St Peter, Buckinghamshire

If you are lost and seeking directions in a rural village but shops are closed for lunch, look for a hair salon as they are always open and most helpful.
        Mrs L Baker, Altrincham, Cheshire

Pets

As dogs cannot digest carrot, you can help your dog to lose weight by reducing the normal, daily food ration slightly and replacing the deficit with raw carrot.

Elizabeth Shaw, London

However tempting it is to do it, do not feed your dog chocolate. All but the chocolate specially made for dogs is poisonous in any quantity.

Mrs E Avery, Maidstone, Kent

ဆ

To encourage cats to eat their worming pills, serve the food hot and the pill chilled. It disguises the taste.

J Norton, Thirsk, North Yorkshire

To feed a pill to a cat successfully, crush it into some butter and smear it on to a paw. The cat will then lick herself clean.

Mrs S E Atkinson, Ashbourne, Derbyshire

To encourage a dog to eat a tablet, hide the pill in a piece of semi-soft cheese. The cheese will stick to the pill and hold it firmly, unlike small pieces of meat and similar titbits.

Angela Bennett, London

ဆ

Put the left-over bits of wool from your knitting basket in your hamster cage – it makes ideal bedding for him.

Celia Sharman, London

During wet weather, line your dog's basket with newspaper before taking him out for his walk .It will soon absorb the wet from his coat, and can then be disposed of, saving you the trouble of washing endless smelly dog blankets.

Amanda Warwick, Saffron Walden, Essex

To stop painful ice-balls forming between the pads of your dogs' paws when walking in snow, smear them with petroleum jelly before going out.

Mrs Elizabeth Talbot, Altrincham, Cheshire

To protect a dog's foot bandage from the wet, apply one of the rubber soled, cloth shoes designed for babies.

Elizabeth Shaw, London

Get two lengths of dog-lead from one: buy a heavy-duty split-ring, and attach it to the loop of your dog's lead. When required, halve the lead's length by simply attaching the clasp to both the split-ring and the collar's D-ring.

Elizabeth Shaw, London

⁓

When you are ready to replace the brush section of your electric toothbrush, use the old one for cleaning your dog's teeth.

C Townsend, London

When bathing your dog, shampoo and rinse his head last. He won't shake water all over you if his head is dry.

J Thomas, London

Fit a piece of fine netting over the head of your pet's brush, pushing it down into the bed of the bristles. When you have finished grooming, simply lift off the net and it will take all the hair with it.

J Macdonald, Great Notley, Essex

147

After grooming the cat or dog, put the fur on the bird-table for the birds to use as nest-lining.

M A Love, London

If your long-haired cat has a small area of matted fur, apply a smear of butter to the tangle and she will lick it out.

Mrs V Warwick, Borehamwood, Hertfordshire

Let your birds trim their own claws: wrap each perch in fine sandpaper secured with string.

C Townsend, London

By cutting the bottom off a plastic, one-litre juice carton, you have a disposable pooper-scooper complete with handle.

Mrs Audrey Leyfield, Frome, Somerset

Use the scented bags (designed for disposing of nappies) to pick up after your dog.

Elizabeth Shaw, London

When clearing up after your dog in your garden, pick up the faeces with an old trowel and dispose of the it by putting it down the lavatory; it is more hygienic than filling your dustbin.

A Vincent, Edinburgh

Fed up with plastic cat-litter scoops snapping or being too inflexible? Buy a stainless steel fish-slice and hammer it into a slightly concave shape. It lasts forever and is easily cleaned.

A P Howard, Stockton on Tees, Cleveland

ဆ

When your bitch comes in heat, rub her hind-quarters with oil of cloves: would-be suitors will show little interest.

D Baker, Edinburgh

Oil of cloves applied to ground-level sections of wooden furniture will discourage puppies from chewing them.

Mrs Prudence Holland, London

If your dog urinates on the carpet, do not use pine-scented disinfectant to clean up: it will attract the dog back to the spot and tempt him to repeat the misdemeanour.

S Murray, Whitstable, Kent

When your dog rolls in something disgusting, apply tomato juice to the offending area and rinse. The odour will vanish.

Mrs J Kefford, Hinton St George, Somerset

ဆ

A damp sponge wiped over upholstery will collect pet-hairs more easily than a vacuum-hose.

Cindy Wolfenden, Southampton, Hampshire

Pet-hairs can be removed from carpet by stroking the fibres firmly with a rubber-soled shoe. (The job's even simpler if the shoe happens to be on your foot!)

N D Hardie, London

ဆ

To stop your pet becoming anxious when you are away, leave a garment smelling of you on a favourite sleeping spot.

N Friendlay, Walton-on-Thames, Surrey

Acknowledgements

This book could not have been compiled without the help of many readers of *The Daily Telegraph*. They include:

Irene Ainsworth, K Alder, Kate Alldis, Mrs Eileen Avery, Mrs J Avery, Mrs D Alexander, Graeme Alexander, Miss P M Alexander, Mrs John Allen, Mrs A R Anderson, Ms M Anderson, Mrs B Andrews, D R Andrew, G J Andrews, Mrs Patricia Andrews, Christopher & Elaine Ashby, J Ash, R H Ashby, Mrs P Ashley, M E Ashmore, Mrs A Ashworth, Hannah Atkins, Mrs S E Atkinson, Robert Austin, D Baker, Mrs L Baker, P J Baker, Hannah Balfour, Mrs G H Ball, Mrs J F Ball, F Barker, Linda Barker, Harry Barnes, Mrs Mary E Barnett, D Barnham, Mrs P Barnham, Mrs C Barnes, Mrs Agnes Barr, K D Barritt, Mrs V Barratt, Mrs Esme Barton, C F Baum, Leslie Baverstock, L Beilby, Joy Bell, Angela Bennett, Miss T Bennett, Mrs S Bent, A A Berry, Mrs D Berry, V I Bettany, Mrs J Bickley, Mrs A Billimoria, R D Bingham, Mrs C Birchenough, Miss J Blackley, Sybil Bleach, L B Bloom, Mrs L Boardman, R K Bobal, Mrs I Boden, Kate Bogle, D K Bonnett, Jane Booth, Mrs E Bostock, Penelope Bourgeois, Mrs L Bowring, Mrs P M Braddell, Mrs L Bradley, Ms H Brierley, J A Briggs, Mrs J A Bristow, Mrs K Brock, Muriel Brocklehurst, Mrs F Brojer, Jennifer Bromley, Mrs N Brookes, Colin Brooks, Mrs Karen Brown, Mrs C Buckell, Caroline Buddery, Mrs S Bunn, Raymond Burger, Miss Kate Burgess, Ruth and Alice Burkitt, Mrs J Burley, J Burns, Mrs A Burrell,

Acknowledgements

Mrs E E Busby, Mrs S G Butcher, Miss J Butler, P Butt, Mrs J Buttery, Mrs E M Caldecott, D Calderbank, Mrs E Campbell, Mrs T Cann, Mrs P Cant, Eileen Caren, Mrs A M Carfoot, H J Carlo, Christine Carpenter, J Carrier, J Carriss, D L Carter, Gladys Carter, Ms Joan Carter, Mrs M A Carter, P Carter, Mrs E B Cartmell, Barbara Cartwright, Mrs E Casement, Elizabeth Cate, J Cater, Mrs L A Catling, Pam Chadwick, Mrs P Child, Mrs J M Chohan, Carolyn Choong, H Chotoye, Mrs E A Churn, Elizabeth Clarke, Charles Cleall, Mrs D Clements, Mrs J Coals, Mrs M Coates, Alice Coffey, Mrs J Coker, Simon Cole, Mrs J Coleman, Mrs K Conn, Mrs J Connell, Mrs G Cook, Mrs Jane Cook, Mrs M Cooke, Mrs M Cooper, Mrs D M Coote, Mrs R Coote, Susan Cornelius, Kathy Corteen, Miss A Cottier, Mrs J Cowdrill, Mrs B Cox, F I Cramp, Carole Cronin, K Crookhall, Mrs T D Crossland, Peter J Cullis, Leonard Cumming, Kirsty Currie, Susan Custance; Mrs J Dalamine, Miss D Davidson, Ian Davidson, Mrs Jean Davidson, Mrs L Davie, Mr & Mrs Davies, Miss A C Davies, Mrs M Davies, Reg Davies, Linda Davis, Mrs P M Davis, J W Dawn, K Denby, Hilary Derouet, Miss B Dorf, Elizabeth Douglas, Katherine Douglas, Mrs S Dowle, Mrs Dora Doyle, J Doxat, Mrs Clare Drewett, Mrs P A Duff, Mrs D S Dunford, Jane Dunning, Geraldine Dyke, J Dyke; Mrs Irene Eade, A Ealand, Gillian Eccles, Mrs I M Edgington, J Edward, Carol Edwards, C W Edwards, K M Egleston, Mrs B J Emmett, Rosemary Eustace, Linda Evans, Mary Falconer, Constance Falwasser, A A Faucheux, Margaret Fearn, Stephen Fessey, Steven Fessey, Mrs M Finch, Mrs V Findlay-Wilson, M A Firth, Cynthia

Fisher, Mrs E Fisher, Mrs E M Fisher, Rita Fitzmaurice, Mrs F M Fletcher, Hornsea, Mrs Hetty Fletcher, Karen Fletcher, Miss Sandra Ford, Mrs M Forsyth, Mary Elizabeth Forsyth, Ms P Fox, K Fricker, N Friendlay, D Fulford, Mrs W E Fuller, Mrs Mary Furneaux; Mrs J Gain, D Galler, Valerie Galler, B Gandy, Mrs Fay Gardiner, Mrs K Gibbard, John Gibbens, Freda Gibson, Brian Gilbert, Camilla Gilbert, Caroline Gilbert, Michael Gilligan, Mrs J C Gingell, Mandy Glancy, Mrs Pat Godleman, Mrs A Goodacre, C M H Goodman, Miss Pat Goodey, J Gostelow, Janet Gould, Mrs M W Grayburn, Silverdale, D B Green, F Green, Mrs J Green, Mrs J A Green, K Green, Sheila Green, Mrs B Greenshields, Mrs P A Gregory, Mrs C E Greville, Jill Griffiths, M Grummell, Mrs Ann Gwyther; Mrs B Haddon, Paula Hagerty, Mrs D Haines, Mrs N Halfhide, B J Hall, Stella Hall, Veronica Hall, Dr S E Halliday, Carolyn Hallinger, Geoff B Hamer, Mrs E Hamilton, D Hancock, Mrs Amina Hannam, N D Hardie, Patricia Hardie, Mrs Harding, R Harding, R & I Harding, G Hardwick, Mrs L Hargrave, Mrs B Hargreaves, M J Harley, Antony J Harper, Cedric Harris, Mel Harris, R Harrison, V A Harrison, E Hart, Rosanne Haselden, Mrs P J Hatton, Mrs M Haworth, Roger Hayes, Ben Heap, Mrs A Heath, G Heath, Mrs B Heathcote, T H Hughes, A Henderson, Mrs L Henderson, Lorraine Hepburn, Mrs D Hill, Joan Hill, Richard E Hill, Miss L C Hinton, Helen Hirst, Peter Hitchings, V Hitchman, Katherine Ho, A Hodson, Anthea Hodson, Mrs F Holbrook, Mrs F Holbrook, Mrs T E Holden, Mrs Prudence Holland, Mrs L P Holliday, Mrs K Hoole, M Hooper, Mrs P Hope, George Hopwood, A P

Howard, S D Howard, Mrs Gwen Howell, I E Howell, M Hubling, Brenda Hughes, Mrs Iris Hughes, Miss M Hume, F Humphreys, Carol Hunt, Mrs M Huntington, Miss E M L Hyatt OBE; Margaret Igglesden, Mrs Diana Irwin, Mrs J M Irvin, Ms M Irwin, Philip Irwin, P Jackson, A James, Ray James, Mrs V Janin, Jonathan Jarvis, Valerie Jenkins, Olive Jeram, Miss H Johnson, Mrs B Jones, J Jones, Judith Jones, Mrs L Jones, Mrs S Jones, Sue Jones, Ted Jones, Charlotte Joseph, Angela Joslin, Mrs M Joyce, B Katz, Mrs D Kazana, Mrs A Keates, Mrs J Kefford, Mrs Gill Kelly, Pauline Kelly, J G Kendall, W A Kennett, Mrs G Kershaw, Mrs L Kettle, Pam Kilbane, Ben King, Kathryn King, S Kingman, Ms E Patricia Kingswell, Peter S Kirk, E Knight, Mrs J Knight, Mrs S Knight, Janine Kotas, C M Kraemer, Tim La Haye, Catherine Lacey, Patricia Laing, Mrs J Laity, Mrs Josephine Lane, James Lark, Susan Latimer, Miss D Law, Rachel Lawrence, R Lawler, John Lawrence, Jack Leaman, Mrs Barbara Lebbon, Mrs Mary Leeland, Trudie Leibling, Jean Lepla, Jayne Lester, P K Lewis, Audrey Leyfield, Mrs J Leyfield, Mrs J Lidbrooke, Mrs M D Lintin, R Linton, Mrs T Linton, Mrs N Little, J Rogers, Warren Little, D Lloyd, Mrs M Lloyd, Mary Lloyd, Mrs M Lockett, Karen Logan, Sylvia Logan, Helen Love, M A Love, M Lovemore, M L Lucas, N Lucas, Mrs Pamela Luck, Mrs U Luton, S N MacArthur, J Macdonald, E MacSween, Ellie MacIsaac, Mrs D Major, L Major, Sally Major, Emily L Mallard, Norma J Mallory, Mrs K Manley, Deborah Mann, Christine Manton, Heather Marks, Miss E K Marriott, A E Marsden, Ann Marshall, G Marshall, Mrs E Martin, Mrs I G Martin, Mrs Y Martin, Mrs

---

L Mason, Barbara Masters, Mrs Mary Mathias, Mrs Maxwell-Irving, Ron Mayers, Sarah Mayhead, K M McCarthy, Megan McConnachie, Eithne McCormack, J McDonald, Ms N McDonald, Cheryl McKeracher, C McKillop, Ms C McManus, James McMinn, Alice McNally, Pat McNeil, John McQuade, Lynne McQuade, Mrs Joan Mead, C Medcalf, B A Mellor, Gill Merritt, John Miles, Mrs Miller, Mrs J Miller, Doreen Mitchell, Miss S Moelwyn-Hughes, Miss B A Moore, R Moore, Patricia Morley, Mrs Carolyn Moore, M S, Mrs M Moran, Mrs P Moren, Mrs E Morgan, G Morgan, Mrs L M Morgan, Mrs J P Morris, Mrs S Morton, Mrs J Moss, Mrs S M Moss, Angela Moules, Isobel Moules, L Moxen, M S, John Mulliner, Mrs S Mullinger, W D Murgatroyd, Mrs C Murray, S Murray; Mrs B Naylor, Mrs C M Naylor, Vera Naylor, R D Nelson, Mrs Marion Newman, D Norman, J Norris, J Norton, S Norton, Eileen Nunn, S O'Dwyer, Mrs A Oliphant, Mrs A Oliver, Mrs A O'Neill, Lyn Orton, Bert Orwin, Mrs E L Orwin, Mark Osborn, Mrs M J Osman, Mrs Maureen O'Sullivan, S Overell, Heather Owen, Mrs M Owen Mrs D Page, C M Page-Turner, Guy Parker, W Parkes, Claudia Parkinson, Sarah Parkinson, Miss Manjula Passey, J Pattison, Angela Pavry, Mrs G Payne, Mrs Sandra Payne, Mrs Gillian Pearce, J Pearson, Winifred Peden, Julia Peduzzi, Mrs J Peek, E Pembroke, Mrs A Penney, B Percy, R Phellas, Mrs M Pickles, Mrs D Pickthall, John Pilgrim, J D Pilling, Irene Pitt, Veronica Potter, Robin C Potts, Mrs D Pover, Mrs P B Prabhu, Alan Price, Mrs J Price, Sarah Price, Mary Priest, Mrs M D Priestley, Charlotte Primrose, Mrs Chloe Purton, Mrs B Purvis, Miss G

F Rae, J Rawlin, J C Reed, C Reeves, Mrs N Reynolds, Brian Richards, H T Richards, Mrs P Richards, S Richardson, Joy Ricketts, P Riley, J Rippon, Mrs A G Roberts, Mrs J Roberts, Mrs J Roberts, P Roberts, Mrs H Robinson, Martin W Robinson, Miss J Roche, John Roger, Mrs D Rogers, Mrs Freda Roles, R S Rossant, J Rothwell, Audrey Routledge, J Royle, M Royle, John Rudkin, Mrs B Ryder, Judith Rydings, M Saarto, Mrs P Sargent, Ursula Sargeson, Mrs A Sawyer, E Scott, Susan Seabrook, Mrs J Seed, Jenny Selby-Green, M Seller, R A Selway, B Semple, L F Shapton, Bob Sharpe, Elizabeth Shaw, Enid Shaw, John H Shaw, Emily E M Shaw-Hardie, Mrs Alma Shell, Mrs S Shepherd, P M Sheridan, P Sherley, Mrs J Shone, Mrs J Sim, Mrs J Simkins, Dennis Simmonds, V Simmons, David Sinclair, James Slater, Carol Small, A Smith, A K Smith, Mrs D K Smith, Mrs E Smith, Felicity Smith, Mrs G H Smith, Mrs G R Smith, Ms J Smith, Mrs J Smith, Ms Jennifer Smith, Linda Smith, Mrs Margaret Smith, R A Smith, R F Smith, Sheila Smith, Mrs M Snapes, Mrs M Snell, Paula South, E Spencer, Mrs J Robert Spencer, Mrs J Spry, A Stacke, Mrs Margaret Standerline, M Standing, Irene Starr, J Stewart, Miss J E Stiles, V Stirzaker, Mrs Morag Stobbart, G Stone, Jane Stones, Mrs N H Strathern, Mrs I Straw, Richard Straw, Patrick Sullivan, M H Surridge, J Swindin; Mrs Elizabeth Talbot, Mrs C Taylor, C J Taylor, Veronica Taylor, R T Temple, Vivienne S Tennant, Miss A Thomas, J Thomas, Mrs W H Thomas, B Thompson, Hythe, Mrs G Thompson, Mrs Maureen Thurston, Mrs J Tilbury, F Tindale, D Fulford, Mrs A Tiney, C Townsend, Mrs B Tracken, Nigel Trapp, Mrs C Tulett, M J

Tunnicliffe, Shirley Van der Beek, Paul Vines, Mrs R Vowles, G Wagstaff, Mrs J M Wagstaff, Rugby, Mrs Walker, Claire Walker, I Walsh, M A Walsh, N M Walsh, Stella Walton, Mrs J Warner, Eira Warren, Amanda Warwick, Mrs V Warwick, Mrs J P Waters, V Warner, G Watson, Mrs B Watts, Mrs M Webster, S Webster, Susan Webster, Derby, Mrs M A Webster, C G Welborn, Mrs V M Wetherall, Julia Wheatcroft, J Whelan, Mrs K L White, Mrs L G White, Carolyn Whitehead, Mrs L Whittle, S Whittle, Frances Wilder, J E Willdig, Mrs E Williams, Emma Williams, Hazel Williams, Mr & Mrs I L Williams, Mrs J Williams, Mary Wilmot, E Wilson, Miss M Wilson, Midge Wise, Mrs J E Wolfe, Jennie Wolfe, Mrs P H Wolfe, Cindy Wolfenden, Mrs J J Wolgan, Mrs J Wood, M Wood, Paula Wood, Dorothy Woods, Mrs W M Woolman, Mrs J Worthington, Neil Wraigh, Mrs Helen Wren, Mrs K M Wren, Mrs Jill Wright, Madeleine Wright, Richard Wyndham, Mrs M Yendall, Mrs Diane R Young, J Young, J R Young.

ॐ

Every effort has been made by the Publishers and *The Daily Telegraph* to contact each individual contributor. If any tip has appeared without proper acknowledgement, the Publishers and *The Daily Telegraph* apoloogise unreservedly. Please address any queries to the editor, c/o the Publishers.

Index

Index

Index

The

Elements

of

Typographic

Style